Aksana Palevich was born and raised in a small village in Belarus. By the age of 13, she had moved to the capital city of Minsk together with her family. After fruitless efforts of getting admitted to the National State University, she took a two-year higher education program at Minsk Technical College. Those were hard financial times, so instead of continuing her education further, she started an early career working as a personal assistant in a large transportation company in Belarus.

Searching for the means to establish and develop herself, she took the risk of moving abroad alone with just ten dollars in her pocket and a bag of clothes. The power and will to survive made her impossible dreams possible. She eventually graduated from the Copenhagen Business School, obtaining her bachelor and master's degrees with top grades. Battling a very tough job market competition for graduates, she successfully went through a lengthy assessment process and received her first real job offer at one of the top five consulting firms in the world. In 2007 she started her fast-paced career in Accenture Management Consulting, working long hours and flying long distances. Aksana worked with multinational global companies for more than a decade, and recently became an independent consultant, running her own consultancy company. She continues to challenge herself, reaching impossible goals, discovering new ways of living, learning and enjoying life at the fullest.

Aksana currently lives in Copenhagen, Denmark, together with her daughter, Maali Mogensen.

Aksana Palevich

THE TEN-DOLLAR DREAM

AUSTIN MACAULEY PUBLISHERS™

LONDON • CAMBRIDGE • NEW YORK • SHARJAH

A CIP catalogue record for this title is available from the British Library.

ISBN 9781398430815 (Paperback)
ISBN 9781398430822 (Hardback)
ISBN 9781398430846 (ePub e-book)
ISBN 9781398430839 (Audiobook)

www.austinmacauley.com

First Published (2021)
Austin Macauley Publishers Ltd
25 Canada Square
Canary Wharf
London
E14 5LQ

There have been many people who contributed to this book, such as my family, my friends, my neighbours, my colleagues, partners and clients – many people I love and admire. Thank you for being a part of my life and part of who I am today.

Thank you to Nete Schmidt for reading the early version of the project months ago, providing valuable feedback and most importantly, believing that my story would reach many hearts.

A special thank you to Jane Friedman for providing a list of recommended resources, to Lisa Ellison for being a very thoughtful and supportive coach. Thank you to Melissa Wuske for a tremendous job with line editing, structural changes and valuable comments.

Thank you to David Wogahn for publishing and distributing this e-book. And, last but not least, a big thank you to Jim Symcox, for correcting my, at times, unclear messages and sentences, grammatical mistakes and for making my story easy to read. As an unknown author, I struggled to find a trusted partner, who could help me to release a printed version of the book. After months of searches, I received a positive response from Austin Macauley Publishers Ltd. I am thrilled, happy and thankful to them for helping me take the final exciting ride of the book journey and have an old-fashioned printed book in my and my readers' hands soon.

Without your help, it would not be the most beautiful life experience. Thank you.

– Aksana

To Maali:

Maali, my angel, becoming a mother and welcoming you to this world was the last missing motivation for this book.

You are my one and only miracle that inspires me to reach the sky and to touch it. I am looking forward to our life journey together and my love for you is unconditional. I love you very much. I don't think I realise it myself. You are in my soul, my heart, my body, my smile and my everything. And you are my pumpkin girl.

Mama

Table of Contents

Introduction   13

Living What I'd Learned   15

The Start   18

The Route   27

The Highway   33

The Coffee Break   41

The City   47

The Sightseeing   55

The Danger   59

The Escape   64

The Repair   68

The Fuel   74

The Engine   81

The Gearshift   86

The Crossroad   91

The Turn   95

The Discovery   100

The Walk   105

The Dreamland   **110**

The Destination   **115**

List of My Life Lessons   **120**

Live and love your own dream.
Nothing will ever break the human ability to fight.

Introduction

All you need to establish your own unique dream is yourself. I hope this book gives you inspiration. Because nothing is more important than the feeling of the most powerful vibe on Earth: Our human life.

I was born in a small village in Belarus and went to school during the times of communism. It was a time when children had access to many development activities like theatre, dance and music classes free of charge. And it was a time when we all had to be equal; there was no room to stand out from the crowd. We all had to follow one direction: The Soviet way. I, no matter which route my life takes, will always be proud of one thing: No one bought my dream for me; I worked hard to reach all my victories. I was not alone though; people challenged me, believed in me and inspired me to make impossible things possible.

In many ways, my story begins on April 2, 2000. I was young and naive, stepping off the plane at Copenhagen airport. I was coming from a beautiful Soviet-influenced Belarus to the freedom of speech of Denmark. I was taking the first steps in daring to change my life and build a dream from nothing but drive, desire and courage. What followed that day were the choices, experiences, victories, disappointments, struggles and celebrations, that became the story of my life. I was fearless, independent yet vulnerable and scared. I learned so much along the way – lessons that I know can help you find the power to realise your unique dream.

In the process of building my dream from scratch, I remained kind and grateful for all life's opportunities. I remained a winner and I still fight for a better future for myself and the people I love. Do not let money or power overshadow the people around you. Look for people and see them. Look for real values and true healthy relationships. Look for compassion and help the ones you can. Help save children and help save our planet. Help save yourselves from being hurt and vulnerable.

Stay strong. Stay calm. All your wishes will come true when your eyes are looking at the right elements. All you need is yourself. Decide today to stop chasing a theoretical dream and start living the fruits that you can grow and pick yourself. You will be amazed by the energy and power inside of you. You will shine and people will notice it. And when you shine, the whole world will dance around you.

Living What I'd Learned

True values around me.

This book was almost done when the whole world started closing down and the coronavirus took over the minds of the people across the entire globe. The virus was spreading fast and the number of countries impacted was increasing at a rapid rate. Just like many of you, I started to worry, think of possible impacts, follow the developments of such an unpredictable situation and think of my family's well-being. When the situation reached its height in Denmark, I ended up in a national lockout with my six-year-old daughter and my stepmother who was visiting us from Belarus at that time.

On the first evening of the lockout, millions of thoughts raced through my mind. I went to my office one last time the day after, leaving my daughter at the apartment with my stepmother to prepare for when the country completely shut down. Already during that morning bicycle ride to work, I had seen the empty streets. I had to support my company by creating the lockout communication and ensure that my colleagues were safe. I knew that was the last day before I would be back in the office again. When work was settled and I was biking back home, I could not stop thinking about how happy I was going back home to the two people I love deeply, my daughter and my stepmother. There was a strong wind that day; I had to stop and walk pulling the bicycle along. It felt like the longest trip ever. But I was going home to my loved ones and I was truly happy to know I would be home soon. I stopped to buy groceries. The stores were empty of bread, meat and dairy products but I managed to buy the necessities and when I finally made it home, I gave all my love to my girls and we had a long evening discussing everything else but the corona situation.

And there was only one big concern I had, how to safely send my stepmother home to Belarus? After spending countless hours on the phone with the governmental authorities, hotlines and health organisations, we organised the trip back home for my stepmom. It was a long day of travel for her and the longest day of my life waiting for the news that she had safely made it home. But she did. Our hero. After the two weeks of home quarantine in Belarus, she remained healthy and I truly hope that it would stay that way. Most importantly, she managed to get home just like I did, cycling home after the office, thinking of anything else but how to get home.

Eventually, my stepmother crossed three borders between Denmark, Lithuania and Belarus to make it home safely at the age of 77, staying cheerful, strong and positive. In many ways the days of the lockout seemed pretty normal. I could manage my remote work, my daughter's remote activities and many of my volunteer tasks well during the days of quarantine. Both my daughter and I adjusted quickly to the new remote ways and our new daily routine. Every day during the lockout, I tried to keep my daughter energised and to be her only best friend. But one evening she was so sad because she had no friends to play with and she cried. I cheered her up saying that she always had me and I could be any friend she wanted me to be. I realised that was the golden time for me to focus on my family, the people around me, the values I live and the values I hope my daughter will follow. It was a golden time for me to stop rushing to everything in the morning and have time to really say a good morning to my daughter, to stop buying things that I really did not need, to spend time going over every single corner of my life evaluating what it was that I really wanted from the future and what I really desired.

It was time to live out the values that I'd learned throughout life, the lessons I share in this book.

The coronavirus situation makes all of us evaluate our real true presence and existence. The sad part is that the corona times came with a very heavy price, the lives of many people.

There will be losses in everything. Loss of human lives, economies, loss of mental stability and the desire to live. But we will manage. We will manage not only the coronavirus. We will manage the many other challenges of our lives as long as we fight for ourselves for the people we love and never stop believing in our human abilities to survive and keep a keen eye on the true values around us.

May my story energise you and make you stronger. Now in the corona times or in any other difficult situation, whatever it might be.

The Start

Keep your wishes alive and don't stop dreaming.

I stood in the middle of Copenhagen airport, looking at the arrivals signs, scared as a little girl and afraid of everything that I was about to see and experience. A girl born in a small village in Belarus packed her clothes and books and left for Denmark for an entire year at the age of 23, not knowing where she was going or who she was meeting. What she did know was that her long-held childhood fantasy and belief in a dream was about to happen. She had never stopped believing that she could transform her dream into a true reality through the power of visualisation.

The power of the wishes that a person's mind can capture is endless. Catching an idea, contemplating and eventually realising it is an enormous life skill. This power comes through visualisation. This kind of visualisation has no connection to meditation or the valuable mind-mapping techniques used in the business and spiritual worlds today to find the true answers to many of life's challenging situations. A powerful visualisation is a simple, maybe even primitive, lifelong belief that the things that we want to achieve will always come true if we keep on having visual images in our minds about how to get to that desired stage. It is a visual projection of our future, our state of mind focused on where we want to go and what we want to achieve. It is our fantasy that is turning into a strong belief in what we want to see in front of us.

The power of dreaming big and imagining the future was why I risked moving to a country with no money, no friends, no family and no security. That vision about the way to a better future and bigger results has been the driving force in me ever since I was a child and the lessons that I had learned so far made me believe that our dreams can be developed from scratch as long as we believe in our inner human motivation. That self-belief is free of charge and the vision of our valuable dreams is something we can remember at any time to challenge our surroundings to make that image alive.

I have had many visions, wishes and desires and I reached almost all of them. Not overnight, of course but over many years of having lots of fantasies and powerful thoughts. This is actually quite extraordinary but my very childish idea to move to another country and conquer the world came from the time when I was very small. It's not that I did not have a good childhood. I had a great big family. Often, I was longing to spend more time with my parents. But given the fact that we were eight kids, running around the village and teasing each other, my childhood was filled with lots of space for myself and my thoughts. I was a very independent girl, ever since I went to school and I loved trying many things on my own without the help of my parents, sisters or brothers. I lived in a big house with my family, ate our own fresh food, had tons of friends on the streets and a good community around. Yet something was missing. I yearned for something new that I had never experienced before. I was always searching for new discoveries because everything unknown, foreign and inaccessible tempted my childish mind. The reason I was tempted by the unknown only came with time. I only understood this desire when I ended up alone in a foreign country and I found out who I truly am.

When I was a kid, a radio that could receive foreign music was a luxury thing. To hear 'The Beatles' or 'Michael Jackson' was almost impossible. Many things were forbidden at that time in the Soviet Union and finding a channel that could receive foreign songs was almost impossible. My dad was excellent at his work, so he often earned gifts from work for his achievements. He was often pictured on the local 'Wall of Fame' together with other high performers. That was the way to reward top workers during the Soviet Union times. Passing by that wall, I would proudly say to everybody around me that there was a photo of my dad on that wall – my great and hardworking dad; I love you deeply for you being you.

Once my dad brought a radio home as a reward, it was a fancy radio that could find some strange channels with somewhat weird foreign music. I was so fond of that radio that I would hide it between the blankets and turn it on quietly after we were supposed to be asleep. It was a magic piece of technology that gave, both me and my siblings, so much joy. We would listen to the radio and would even try to sing together in Russian trying to mimic the English, not knowing the words but pretending that we sang all the songs correctly. I was around seven or eight years old at that time and already I had created colourful fantasies about living in foreign countries and speaking other languages. I would often imagine that I could freely have a conversation with a foreigner, travel to any country that I wanted and discover beautiful places that I had never visited before. I would dream of a life where I would not depend on my parents and could do anything I wanted and build my life from scratch.

Lesson 1: Don't ignore your childhood wishes and interests. They are the key to understanding and developing your potential. Understand that potential and develop it. If it is hard to detect that potential yourself, talk to your parents, siblings, friends or anyone who knows and cares about you.

I first travelled abroad when I was 11 years old. My brother and I spent a month living with a host family in Germany. *What strange people they were,* I thought. They had way too many rules in the house and they were scared if we ate green apples from the trees in their backyard. They had regular meals at exactly the same time and they would keep an eye on us all the time. I was very curious to understand their routines, what they ate and how they spoke. We got our first stereo recorder as a gift from our host family and we tried to record our voices. We laughed so much because we could not understand why our voices sounded weird and my brother kept on saying that there is no one else in the room, so the recorded voices must indeed be ours. That trip to Germany was the first little touch of the world abroad and the first little inspiration for me. And the voice recording was my first childish reflection on who I was and why I loved to explore life in a very different environment – because I realised that the way I sound, act and live every day is a long, exciting and never-ending unread book. I realised then that I have so much to discover. That simple voice recording gave me an enormous desire to learn more about what I can live and experience and who I can become in the future.

Music touches me deeply and I can never resist its magic. When we returned from Germany, I borrowed as many cassette tapes as I could so I could play them on my stereo. It didn't matter if I didn't know the words or what the songs meant. I was in love with all that foreign music. I think my first cassette tape was an '80s' disco hits volume and maybe that's why I will always be dancing to that energetic music at the age of 100. I didn't speak English at that time, so I could only remember a few names. Madonna, The Jacksons, Whitney Houston and Bon Jovi had a big impact on my development. I discovered I liked pop music mixed with heavy rock. Diversity in music and a strong belief in my dreams were the foundation for my life journey to come.

Music lifted my desire to dream, dare and explore and my mind began creating a fairy tale about a faraway country. While listening to the music, I dreamed of living a good life and getting the things that my parents couldn't give me (like new clothes, so I would not need to wear my sister's used dresses or my own bedroom so I could listen to my music and have some private time). I was also dreaming of becoming the best in everything I did and everything I could do. I liked being a free spirit and I liked mastering new subjects. I was never good at mathematics but I had a stubborn nature to sit down and learn the equations on my own. I remember that my dad would help me with solving some math equations but with so many children he could not give me much time every day. I dedicated a good amount of time to doing homework alone because of one very simple thing: I hated the feeling of the unknown and I did not want to be the bottom student in the class. I wanted to be prepared, sharp and ready for the next day. And I am sure that this childish dedication and desire to know brought me the images of a better life abroad. At that time, of course, I did not fully realise that I dreamed about living abroad because I went to a Soviet Union-style of school and feelings were not discussed. We were the Soviet children that could not even argue with teachers during classes or discuss problems. We were always told what to do. Deep inside, however, I kept on challenging myself, not knowing the way to my dream and I was preparing myself for some fun and challenging life experiences. And maybe that is why I was eventually much better at English in school than with the Belarusian language.

By the time I went to college, I realised that I really wanted to travel abroad, even if only for a short time. I was so fond of foreign cultures, languages, music and movies that my visualisation of jumping on a plane and landing in a foreign country was developing into a dream – even though it seemed almost unachievable. Leaving Belarus and establishing yourself in another country was a rare thing. Just to receive a visa to travel abroad was a luxury at that time. But my dream felt like a delicate spring flower that I would notice going to school every day. I had very colourful fantasies about the world that was abroad – a world where I would have the possibility of doing what I wanted and of meeting people who are different in colour, background and nationality. I thought that I just needed to find an easy way to move to another country and from the first day there, I would be a happy girl. I would have my basic needs covered, live in a democratic society and have many open doors to establish a good career. I dreamed of a life that would give me the freedom to do whatever I wanted, instead of being told what to do. I wanted many chances to develop my hidden, unused potential and learn about other countries and travel to any place I wanted. It was a true fantasy and absolutely farfetched from reality. But I believed in it and I started thinking about how I could turn my dream into a reality.

My belief in a transformation of my own setting was becoming stronger but I was not prepared for the fact that it would take years before I could even sense the reality of the dream coming true. I chose not to focus on the hard part and I kept on finding ways of getting closer to my dream. I kept on daydreaming about foreign countries and I used any opportunity to practice my English skills with any foreigners I met via friends. To actually meet a foreigner was a rare thing at that time, so any chance I got was a purely magical moment for me. I met many interesting people that gave me ideas on what could be done about my visions. I even accepted advice from my friends, who told me all I had to do was to find a man abroad and marry him. I did consider that option, even down to registering at a marriage agency in Belarus. It was a common practice and I heard many happy-ending stories but I guess I never believed in that path for me. My transformation route turned out to be much more interesting than the fast-track marriage path.

I finished college and started developing my professional life. My biggest education and investment in who I am professionally today happened with the first company that I was employed by in Belarus. It was that Belarusian company, one of the biggest and most successful ones in Belarus, even today; that gave me immense experience on how to work independently, have a high work ethic, always wear appropriate clothes and have strong discipline. I was the face of the company, working as a personal assistant for the top management and I had to be sharp, professional and always on top of my duties. The job was well-paid and I was very proud of having the position at that company compared to the job offers that my fellow graduates had. It was also a means to support both myself and my family and I earned more than my dad did because I had completed higher education. I never mentioned that to my dad; he was a hero for me no matter what his salary level was.

It was a long ride from home to work and one day a female colleague took a seat next to me on the company bus. We chatted about our work and, somehow, we started talking about the possibilities of working abroad. My colleague mentioned the idea of being an au pair, a nanny living in a host family and taking care of the children. It was a possibility to move abroad, try an unknown setting and examine whether I could manage the change. It was a possibility to prove to myself that the visualisation of my long-term wishes could be real – as real as I could see and feel them. After that bus ride, it took me years of paperwork, medical records, interviews and a discouraging amount of waiting time to finally find a host family in Denmark. But it happened. An unrealistic, childish goal turned into a life-changing story. It was my first personal achievement that turned my values upside down and made me believe that anything can happen because I never gave up on seeing and imagining my future ambitions.

Lesson 2: Visualise and keep your ideas tuned, so you keep believing in impossible things and staying focused for years. Visualise how to get to that unreachable point and hold onto your vision. Don't think that all you need is luck to accomplish your dreams. It is hard work. It will most likely not turn out exactly the way you imagined but it definitely will be a very close match or even a much better version of your powerful visualisation.

The Route

Getting rich with empty pockets by investing in the future.

We do not need money and powerful connections to become successful. Success is in our hands, even with empty pockets and no friends. Money can aid success, open doors and broaden our possibilities but money does not make us successful. We can make ourselves successful without money. Money plays a role in making the right life decisions. One of the best choices, where money plays an important role is education. If you need money to get a very good education, work hard to get there and all that hard work will pay off for you in the future. I did that back in 2002. During the first few au pair years, I saved my earnings, so I could go back home and provide more financial security for myself and my family. I did not intend to spend the earnings anywhere apart from Belarus because the resources in Belarus to help my family were limited and I could barely provide any help for my family with the earnings I made back home. The au pair salary was far from an income I could save a lot from, yet it was an amazing chance to start saving, at least in small steps. Each day spent as an au pair was a small milestone for me because I had a fantastic job taking care of the children and I was proud of it. The pocket money I was receiving was a strong symbol that my work was recognised and I deserved to save some money for me and my family in Belarus. I put in almost all the savings I earned as an au pair to cover the costs of my first year of studying in Denmark. The benefit of that decision was endless. It was the best investment ever. I had invested in my education, the biggest asset embedded in me for my entire life.

Lesson 3: Investment in the future and especially investment in your education is the key to a happy and rich life. You will be rich not only in financial terms, even if one day you might earn your millions, which you most likely will – with the right dedication and drive. But you will also be rich inside, knowing that a personal drive and dedication cannot be bought but that the results of what you can learn doing your studies will be remarkable. No one can take education away from you.

Paying that huge fee for my first year of education in Denmark was a very tough choice because my plans for helping my family and establishing myself in Belarus were disappearing. I had worked hard during the au pair years, tired or not, wanting to or not, I always went to work and did the best I could. My ambition was to go back home to Belarus, find a small place to live, stop depending on my parents and stop needing to save for months and months before I could afford a new dress or buy myself a decent lunch at work. I wanted to financially support my family but I had to give up all my plans and hopes for the sake of my education in Denmark. And yet I knew that getting an education was an opportunity I couldn't pass up and, that, in the end, it would be better than the life I'd been dreaming of.

I do not regret a single minute that I invested in my education but I must admit that it was not an easy choice. But I made that choice. I made it being afraid, wondering if I'd finish the education, master academic English, be socially skilled to talk to my classmates and whether I'd understand supply and demand and elasticity curves during my first classes in economics. I struggled to understand the theories of marketing and I was completely lost during the strategy classes, not following a single model due to the language barrier. My social skills were very Soviet; I could not freely speak about my fears when discussing the group work with my teammates. But the choice was done and I had to stick to it.

I was still living with a host family as I had to cover the costs of my education. In the morning, I would take the child I cared for to school, then ride my bicycle to classes. When I got back home, I'd do chores for the host family and in the late in the evening, I spent time doing my homework. I created my own dictionary of unknown words and business phrases and every evening I would go through the entire dictionary memorising the words. I pushed myself to establish connections to non-Russian speaking classmates and I attended very international parties to improve my social skills. I became best friends with some of my classmates and I even cherish and nurture some of those relationships today.

After two years of the everyday commitment to make my education an essential part of who I am, I passed all my exams with top grades; I gave the valedictorian speech at graduation, I got admitted to the Copenhagen Business School. I became an international social girl with friends from all over the world.

Lesson 4: Know your strengths. Think of the qualities that keep you going and make you stubborn, the things that you are most capable of. You know them, I am sure. When you know your ultimate capabilities, you just need to find the last piece: How to utilise your own skills and capabilities correctly. Stick to your decisions. Money can never buy you the power of your own abilities.

Moving completely out of our comfort zones and protected lifestyles can shed a bright light on what we have and how we want to live. The results of even minor changes in our lives can be astonishing. The things we experience during a change – be it reaching great results at school, starting with a risky goal or investing in something that has no definite outcome – will eventually lead to a feeling of immense satisfaction when you achieve success. The feeling of being able to change and challenge the surroundings on my own has become a personal addiction to me. I find so much joy in reaching the impossible, that today I am addicted to my small victories and I hunger for more wins and more ambitious goals.

My victories started all the way back in my childhood when I was afraid of riding a bicycle because I might fall and injure myself. My parents would not allow me to ride an adult bicycle at the age of eight. Out of curiosity I quietly took the bike without their permission. I put it close to a hedge, so I would be able to crawl on the seat and try to move the pedals. After only a few times I fell, then I would get up and try all over again. Eventually, I learned to cycle on my own and it was my secret childhood victory. Growing up and becoming an adult, my victories developed into grander moments and I was content with my decisions. When I was not admitted to the Belarussian State University, a quick solution was to apply for a two-year higher education so I would not lose the entire year of waiting time. I was admitted, even though I only had a few weeks to prepare. I completed my education and I did a brilliant job of getting that first job in the coolest Belarussian Company. The combination of risky decisions, tight deadlines and unachievable goals brought me this victory. And, yes, I enjoyed it to the fullest and I was very proud of it. I wish this feeling for you too because your life will never be boring again. No money will ever buy you the feeling of having the whole world at your feet. That feeling will come when you realise that your actions turn into something very extraordinary, something that makes you feel proud, something that you barely believed you could ever have done. It's the feeling that you're standing in front of a deep ocean and you know how to cross it regardless of how long it takes.

We don't need money to succeed and neither do we need a powerful network to become successful. Power and money are a great cocktail but they really do not create a better life for us. They even might complicate our lives and give us more stress than joy because the power might overshadow the desire and drive to establish the things that we can build independently and the money might provide a false sense of security. I did not have any connections or powerful contacts when applying for au pair positions back in 1998. I spent countless days filling out forms and waiting to hear from potential families. It took over two years before my journey into my new life truly began. My victory didn't arise from powerful connections or money. I had to borrow the money to cover the entire cost of my travel to Denmark. My dream happened because I kept on carrying the responsibility of my own decision to move abroad and to challenge my environment. I accepted an enormous risk – one I wasn't even prepared for. I worked hard every day to achieve my dream and confront my biggest fear of all time: a life in a foreign country that was not a fairy tale anymore. It was real and hard every day and facing those challenges made me believe in my own strengths, abilities and passion to dare and challenge any obstacle that I was facing. It came about because I had a hunger for success with no money, no luck and no family support – nothing but myself.

The Highway

We all need a change.

Every human being is born with amazing qualities. We all have some things in common. Yet we all are so truly different and this never stops amazing me. I know successful people who worked the hard way to get to their successes but I also know people who did not fight enough for things that do not come easy. Some of them are results of a social well-being trap. When a society protects a person as a little lion cub, there is an enormous risk of getting used to that protection. What happens next is that the protection gives a false feeling of safety and opens the door towards a very dangerous belief – that someone else will come and solve every problem – while confidence in their own capabilities starts fading away. Society's protection might eventually turn out to be the only reason why a person wakes up in the morning, brushes their teeth and spends the rest of the day in their safety zone. This sense of protection and security is the only mechanism that works for a person to live through another day. The protection becomes an essential part of human life, completely embedded in the routine, daily chores and settings so that the desire to risk, be bold, try out something new disappears as if it never existed. I don't think any person intentionally chooses to fall into such a trap. It just happens. Intentionally or not, if this happens, the only way out is a change – a fast change before the trap becomes stickier and deeper. If you wake up one day and realise that all you do is a waste of time and effort and you have no desire to try out anything new, risky or challenging, this is a perfect moment to start the makeover and start a change journey. Any person can easily spot the signs that a change is needed by simply looking at their daily routine.

There are so many options to start discovering a life of happiness. I truly believe that the easiest and the quickest change starts with a simple, everyday routine. There are many options and doing something different might cost almost nothing. It can be anything. Wearing the running shoes for the first time and going for a run. Feeling the pain of the first run and getting out of breath. Wanting to stop and quit. Feeling miserable and tired. Eventually reaching the first goal, catching your breath and feeling victorious.

A change can also start in the middle of more complex life situations, be it a career move, the birth of a child or cleaning up of personal worries. I deal with the last one regularly – even today. Sometimes, I worry too much and I need a quick fix to manage and control my worries. When I feel that I worry, I typically start losing my focus. I start forgetting things in the morning; I become irritated and angry in simple situations and feel like crying. With years of mental training, I have learned to detect this feeling in a matter of minutes and my latest quick fix is to move the furniture around in my flat. I purchased small movable items on purpose so that I can quickly rearrange, move or change the colour. I can change the shape, colour or the way a piece of furniture is used and I can make something out of very non-functional pieces like using wine corks to make a picture frame. I remove old things from storage and donate toys, that my daughter does not play with anymore, to charity. When I'm done, I light the candles, switch off the lights, go out on the balcony and look back into my apartment through the window, enjoying the view full of satisfaction with a warm heart and quite an 'I did it' moment.

Change can also start in more complex life situations like a difficult career move or hard personal matters. In this case, a change needs to be well-thought through. In many cases, the change will require an attitude, willingness and the determination to make the difference. A change might mean moving out to the suburbs and away from a busy town, hanging up a career path or taking a direction that you had never thought about before. Even shutting down your phone for the whole day and spending quality time with your family, taking your kids to an orphanage and showing them how to care for others can help solve personal matters. Change is in our hands; it is simple and achievable.

Sometimes a change can take many years. As a teenager in Belarus, I was strangely better at English than Russian. I was fascinated by movies in English. My first movie was 'The Bodyguard' and the first time I saw that movie in its original version, I could hardly follow the plot. At best, I understood 20 percent of the entire movie. I was about 15 years old. It was on videotape, so I saw the movie many times. I had to look up tons of words in a dictionary almost every single minute. And I am not a patient person. A few months after I moved to Denmark at the age of 23, I saw 'The Bodyguard' again and I could understand almost all of it. That was a pure euphoric moment in my life – going from understanding nothing about the movie to understanding almost everything.

Lesson 5: You can be very impatient as a person but once you have a goal, you will not need any tools to train your patience. You just sit down and practice because you want something so badly that your determination beats impatience. The years of hard work, constant change and a great deal of belief will generate results that you will not believe at first. But those will be your results and your small victories.

On April 2, 2000, I stood in the middle of Copenhagen airport after spending an hour searching for my luggage. I was meeting a family that I had never seen before and had only briefly talked to on the phone. I worried the whole flight about how I would manage this life change and I was afraid of all the unknowns I might face. I was not really celebrating the victory of arriving in Denmark. On the contrary, I was so overloaded by the new environment, coming from the capital of Belarus to a small Danish farm, that I spent the first nights in Denmark crying into my pillow and thinking of ways of getting back home. I was alone. Completely alone in a strange country. My only connection to my family was a landline phone. No cell phone, no Skype and no email account. I only had a limited time to talk to my family and even then, I kept all my worries deep in my heart. I did not want to disappoint my family. But the truth is I did not want to disappoint myself.

Lesson 6: There will be times where you feel completely and utterly alone. Hold on.

Life as an au pair was not hard. It was good. The host family I lived with was great and I learned a great deal from them. Especially from that cool woman who picked me up at the airport, to whom I have looked up to for many years since I left that family. It was a great family but I could not share my worries with them. They were strangers. I could not tell them that I was afraid of speaking English and I was absolutely lost coming from the capital of Belarus to a tiny village in Denmark. I could not tell them that even my clothes did not fit their settings. I had nice jackets and high heels in my bag but I really needed a pair of flip flops and shorts.

There were too many things that I could not handle and there was poor, frustrated me in the middle of it all. After tears and many days on an emotional roller coaster, I took charge of my own needs. I came up with a solution for what to do and how to act. I initiated a change and did not wait for someone to help me. I had no strategy on how to fix my own frustration. I simply started changing. I started intensively watch movies in English, reading every single subtitle to understand the plot. I used videotapes at that time, so I would pause and look up unknown words in the dictionary, rewind and start from the beginning. I opened a Hotmail account and started browsing the internet to get connected with other au pairs. I created a list of Danish phrases written with Russian letters so I could communicate with the child I was responsible for. I went shopping after my host family happily supported my decision to change my wardrobe a bit. A few months after I landed in Denmark, I was running around the small town of

Roskilde wearing sporty H&M pants and Nike shoes that felt comfortable enough to walk anywhere. I could pick up Christopher from day-care and I could understand what he was saying to me in Danish.

Lesson 7: Don't wait for the rain of help to be poured on you from the sky. When you are in a huge change process, get things done for yourself. Just do it. No one can do it better than you. And you will enjoy the accomplishment.

I was very proud of two things. First was the decision that changed my life forever and second was the speed with which I adopted that change. Even with my initial difficulties in Denmark, I decided not to go back home to Belarus immediately after the first weeks. I decided to hold on until my body and mind settled down in the new environment. In fact, that and the decision to bring a baby to this world as a single mom are the two choices that I most admire and cherish deeply. I would not be me today if I had not taken those risks and all the consequences that came along with them.

Before I moved to Denmark, I had always thought of myself as a person who had a very hard time adjusting and changing settings. I had a hard time as a kid changing places, crying my heart out for days when my parents put me in a summer camp. I did not like change. And maybe I don't even like it today. But given the situation I was in, I knew that if I did not try to fit myself into the Danish way, I would feel limited and unable to fully function. That is why the speed of my makeover was fast. I did not like change but I had to change. I did not like the new setting initially but I had to face the consequences of my own decision to leave Belarus and come to Denmark. No matter how hard and painful the consequences were, I knew that I was responsible for them.

Lesson 8: Be bold and take a risk. Take on manageable risk. Don't just be a fool putting yourself into a life and death situation. Choose the risks that you know you can handle and not the ones where you would clearly overload yourself. You will know the ones you can handle; you will feel them with your entire body.

Decisions are probably the toughest parts of our lives. You can always seek advice from family and friends and you should. At the end of the day, however, any decision is your own call. I've had many decisions I needed to take on my own since I lost my mother at the age of 13 and ended up living with my sister and a brother, alone in a big house. It was not that my father abandoned us. He just moved with my stepmother a few streets away. They made sure that we had all necessities around the house but they were not there to help me to deal with school problems or fights on the streets. It wasn't that they had bad intentions. They technically could not help. There were eight children in my family and then three more from my stepmother. Eleven of us. My dad could not help me decide how to deal with teenage problems. I had to deal with them myself and I do not even remember how I managed to come up with decisions to the many challenges on my own. What I remember was that I hated the feeling of being helpless and vulnerable, so I would always have a plan of what to do and I would always find a way to defend myself. If somebody hit or teased me at school, I punched back and never gave up fighting for myself.

Lesson 9: Decisions, effort and the consequences of your actions will show the way to reroute your settings. Most importantly, the ability to undergo change will forever mean that you can adjust in any tough life settings. This is the skill that you can carry for life.

The Coffee Break

Personal limits and simple things.

Years ago, I discovered that a recipe for a happy life exists. I needed to find that recipe so I could finally understand what makes me happy and how I could establish a complete list of happy ingredients. Knowing the number of factors and elements contributing to the core of my happy existence was important. But by simply knowing the elements of what makes me happy, I was only halfway to understanding the recipe. The complete palette of those ingredients meant almost nothing because I also needed to know how to apply them in my daily life.

During the fast-paced years of establishing myself in Denmark, I found the recipe because I had dedication and drive and every day I moved at an enormously fast pace. I also found the key ingredients. However, I did not know how to use some of those ingredients wisely. I could potentially use the happy ingredients in a mature way but I think I was afraid. I was scared to end up in very difficult moments. Over the years, though, a fragile and uncertain schoolgirl developed into a young woman, who knew that she simply had to stand up and live her personal values every day, whether it meant standing up for a challenge or making others aware of her personal limits.

In my consulting career, I have met people from different parts of the world and I have worked with many different personalities. On one occasion, many years ago, I learned a great deal about my values and how much I can handle in a tough work situation. It is clearly one of my greatest learning experiences, even though right at that time I was devastated and hurt. I was working as an external consultant and my constant headache, troubles and frustrations were related to one client. As everyone in consulting knows the client comes first. So, really, I had no choice but to keep on working as if nothing was wrong. I did not talk about it and, of course, I did not do anything to protect my personal limits that were clearly overloaded with sleepless nights, constantly thinking, anger and frustration. I had to deliver good consulting work and I had to do it under any circumstances. I looked happy at work but deep inside I was miserable because all I tried to work on, suggest and deliver were not recognised, even after a long time with the client. The problem I was facing was simple. A person that I was dealing with was new to the company and was a master in old ways of doing things. I spent months finding how to deal with the situation and I ignored the limits that I had as a consultant and a human being. Because I did not want to give up, I kept on believing that things would eventually work out.

I did not stand up for myself, most likely because I was very young and I was afraid of losing a fantastic reputation and the top performance that I had at that time. I was not listening to my own discomfort and I did not feel my own needs. Eventually, I broke down in tears during a regular meeting, having reached the final level of my frustration. The day after that episode, I missed my flight going to an important client workshop. I had taken hundreds of flights before and I could not possibly miss that flight. But I did, I had lost the focus needed to be quick, prepared and always at my best at work. This was the culmination for me and I had to figure out what was going on. It took me days, maybe months or even several years after that moment to realise that no matter how tough the work situation, I could never jeopardise my personal, professional and human limits.

Lesson 10: Understanding how we as humans should or should not act is a brilliant lesson. If you do not know your personal limits, study and find them. If you do, stick to them and live up to them. Stick as much as needed and not as much as might seem wanted. Utilise and protect your energy and your mental power, even if you are afraid and uncertain.

Becoming a mom, I realised that protecting my personal values and limits has powerful consequences. Parenting strengthened my ability to sort out unnecessary focus points, not wasting a minute on unnecessary explanations, arguments or conversations. That technique came almost immediately after I rearranged my entire lifestyle, so I would be able to raise my daughter on my own. Focusing on the right elements and at the right moments was a tremendous skill that I had to discover as I became a parent. For example, one day I received a long email that according to the sender was urgent but I eventually answered it many days later. The matter was related to volunteer work and it was not life threatening, so the right time to answer that email was after I had managed my daily chores, went to work, delivered and picked up my daughter from day-care, completed things around the house and, most importantly, had a happy and clear mind to manage my three-year-old, who occupied my day 24/7. By sorting out the unnecessary focus elements of my life, I built up a much stronger meaning of what it means to live a simple life and I learned where energy is needed the most and how my personal limits could remain healthy.

During my childhood, I knew that I needed to speak up and defend others, especially when it came to defending someone who was quiet or weak at school. I tried to defend others as a kid and I still defend the ones who need support. I worked as a volunteer for decades for vulnerable children and families and I helped schools and orphanages around the world collect toys and school materials. I engaged my personal network and I also involved my little daughter in making a difference for almost 100 children in one particular school in Belarus. I did so not because I wanted to have glory or to feel like a hero. I did it because I knew how easy it was to make someone smile and feel important, especially children. It was easy to stand up for the lives of the families and children, for the ones who needed love and care. The lesson I gained through many years was truly simple. I became someone who loves success, career moves, making investments and daring to achieve a lot. But I also became someone who values simple things and simple pleasures, regardless of my income and the number of things I could afford. My lifelong belief in simple things, together with protecting my personal limits, created that final combination of how to use my happy life ingredients every day.

Lesson 11: Find and cherish the elements of life that make you happy and make sure that you really enjoy them. Look for simple values and real triggers of happiness. You have plenty of those around you right now. All you need is to see them and to feel them.

Simple things make me happy. Very happy. Basic values and simple life pleasures are so dear to me that they overshadow very expensive materialistic things. One day I was driving to work on an early winter morning. It was cold but luckily the sun was shining and it looked bright yellow. It had this simple form that I'd seen so many times. I stopped at a streetlight, looked around and noticed that the sun was reflecting in the right-side mirror. It was a simple, round and yellow present every day. That basic image of the sun made me smile all the way to work. I was almost naive and childish to realise so late that the simple sun had an enormous power over me. But it was definitely not too late to admit that I love simple things because I can see and feel them everywhere. It can be the moments when I soak myself in freezing cold water because it makes my body feel fresh and alive and I am thankful every time for having a chance to feel that cold water around me. And it can be the voice of my little daughter asking me if I have seen the fish yet, boosting the child in me who wants to play along, find the fish, make the little princess smile and create fun childhood memories. I love simple things because they make me feel energetic, alive and powerful. That little winter morning the sun that was shining in the mirror; it just reminded me that the simple things were always around me. I just did not see them.

Being so much in love with simple things, I have a hard time understanding why people spend millions competing with one another. I do respect competition and I do not criticise that. Going to many dinners and social events and meeting people from all over the world, I have heard thousands of questions about whether a person has a rich partner or an expensive car or if their kids attend the most expensive private school. The most this and the most that have never synced in my consulting brain, which has an enormous tendency to ask 'why' questions. I never understood that type of competition and I probably never will. It does not make me as happy as basic, real and simple life pleasures.

The City

Keep professional stress out of your home.

Protecting the core in our personal lives is as important as protecting the borders in professional settings. There are and will be thousands of situations in our work life where we see that all our good work is not appreciated or we are tired of work politics. There will be complex problems and many moments when we will feel our high morning energy vanishing the minute, we enter the office. And there will be a dozen reasons why.

We cannot change the fact that we take worries from work and bring a negative vibe back to our homes. Even if we have no intention of doing that, it can happen because we are all influenced by what happens around us during the day. We cannot change that fact but we can instruct our minds to set a shield and practice how to let work politics and stressful events stay at work. I once came home after a hard day at work. I picked up my daughter at a day-care and we came home to our usual routine. Instead of spending time with my daughter, I was looking at my phone and was still checking my emails. Some of those emails were complex but I had to respond fast to close down some confusion. Reading all emails, the level of my frustration was increasing and I needed to focus on a proper way of writing the answers. My daughter needed my attention and she was not getting it. She started crying. I was so overloaded with problems at work that instead of calming her down, I raised my voice and tried to educate her that Mom should not be disturbed and that I had no time to hear her crying. I walked away into another room and it took me a few minutes to understand that the problem was me and not her. It was my focus that was blurry from the things at work that I brought home with me. These few minutes were one of the greatest lessons for me.

I went back to my crying daughter. I hugged her tightly and I apologised. I told her that I had not understood how much she needed me and that she had my full attention. I did not mention how hard my day was or why I reacted the way I did. I did not need to do that. What I needed to do was to leave the work vibe far away from my home and that little person I love. She stopped crying immediately and, in a few seconds,, forgot all about it. But I did not. And I never will.

Lesson 12: We cannot avoid stressful situations at work; they will happen. If you are home after a crazy day at work and act irritated, use your lungs and your mind. Isolate your work problems forever and never bring them home again. Go back to your child, your husband, your loved ones and apologise.

Solving work issues can be a long process. Long because most challenging work situations happen unexpectedly and when we least expect them. It might come through a round of discussions, frustrations and drastically fast conclusions. I have been in some interesting situations, where I thought that the only way out of a conflict at work was my quick resignation. It seemed like leaving the tough situation was the only way to retain my personal dignity, professional pride and most importantly, professional respect. I thought of doing it once but I hesitated and decided to give myself some time to understand what really was happening at work. I had to admit that I was going through a phase of being angry and frustrated. And it was absolutely fine to feel that way. I needed to get over that first reaction to tune my focus and clear my thoughts for a while. I had to do that, so I could understand what was happening and make the best decision to find the way out. I was overloaded with a massive feeling of being helpless and it took some time to figure out the solution. With time, I understood that my feelings were not any different from other people's feelings. We all defend our positions and point of view in the moments of crisis. What differentiates us though is the length of time we bear the frustration and indecisiveness.

Lesson 13: Do not overreact and create unnecessary drama out of tough moments at work. Get a good night's sleep. Think the day after. Focus your thoughts to think of solutions. My grandma used to tell me, "A morning is wiser than an evening."

Remembering the wise words of my grandmother, I had a good and long sleep for the first time in days if not months. I could not switch off thinking about what to do but I tried to leave the problem unattended for some time. It was all worth it. One day, I woke up and decided to look for an optimistic solution, not because I wanted to get out of feeling miserable but because I wanted to find a solution. Fast. In a situation when there is lots of frustration, there is a brilliant solution as well. I thought that I wanted to quit my job immediately but I hesitated. I had a feeling that I wanted to run away to some other place and hide, so no one could find me. But I also knew that there was something else that could explain the discomfort and the explanation could be hidden in my own behaviour. I remembered a moment from my childhood. I was in a third grade at the primary school and you were not allowed to wear earrings till a certain age but I asked my aunt to pierce my ears anyway. As a consequence at school, I was abandoned by almost my entire class and had no one to talk to for weeks until things settled down again. I often sat on my own during classes and I had plenty of time to observe others. That childlike learning gave me a hint about what I needed to do to find the solution to my work problem.

After some weeks of emotional struggle at work, I went into a passive mode, just like the time when I sat alone on a school bench and I started screening my work and my relationships. I noticed that things were functioning in a very unprofessional manner around me. My biggest discovery after several months with that firm was that the company had a long history of old routines, where no one wanted to give up the power they'd gained over many years. The easiest way out of an argument was to blame someone else. And hence, the firm had no space for a person like me, even after spending time and money on hiring me in the first place. I had no chance to contribute to a company that did not recognise passion for change. So our marriage was wrong from the beginning and the relationship was never meant to last.

In the end I had to acknowledge that it was not my battle to win and my professional integrity meant much more than anything else. I concluded that the one and only wise decision would be to leave that company. Not to run like a scared mouse but to walk out gracefully after leaving my personal footprint. I realised I actually had one thing I could do before quitting that job. I could show that anyone can change and adjust to any setting – to act on changes and not discuss changes. I could, with my own behaviour, show that in a world of constant changes, it is a must to adjust and change the old-rooted routines. It is a must to respect each other and it is a must to stop a blaming ping-pong. It takes only one person to initiate a change and I truly wanted to be that person. I wanted to make sure that I left my individual touch about how to stop backstabbing and start adjusting. I did that in many meetings I attended and many projects that I delivered for that company. I was very content with my decision and I put my best efforts into it. And I finally quit that job – in a very calm, elegant and professional manner.

Lesson 14: It does not matter what position you have in a company and it does not matter if you have no formal power to change a complicated situation. What's important is that it can be you who changes the deep-rooted routines or restricted boxes of thinking. Be that person. Speak up even if your employment is at risk.

I always spoke well about that company or any other company I've worked for and I always will. The time that we invest in our professional growth is valuable learning in any setting. The time I invested in that professional experience taught me that I can do anything to initiate a change. I learned that I could leave the firm with dignity and pride. I just needed to stay honest to myself and leave in an elegant manner. Becoming a mother taught me another lesson. I always believed that my full focus was needed in any tough situation and only lately have I understood that there is really no need to spend energy on analysing 100 percent of everything at work, especially when it comes to choices and challenges. There are tons of other jobs out there but the inner power does not change at a particular job; the inner drive and ability remain with us. So if you have decided to invest fully in changing things at work, think of one important limitation: The commitment to solve tough job situations must never enter your home.

My career was important to me at every stage of my professional growth. It still is and always will be till I retire. Even then I would think of running a small store or restaurant. I would need to do something not to get bored and to feel that my professional blood is still circulating in my veins. My career gives me a kick. Without it, I would not be in the place I am today. My professional experiences have taught me so much. And I value and appreciate them enormously. I appreciate every single day that brought me these seas of opportunities. It is very healthy to react to job offers that come along and seize market opportunities, not only when things are tough at work but also as a healthy path to professional self-development. It's always fun to hear and see opportunities. Every job offer deserves consideration and human beings are well suited to employment. My grandmother used to say a job makes a person beautiful and honourable. A job makes a human shine and spark because it challenges and makes them think big. It is a huge respect and honour to have any job, be it as an au pair, a cleaning lady, a consultant or a CEO. We can all find potential in any job or a career move. Big or small potential, it does not really matter. As long as you know that the job you have helps others in their life achievement or journey. An au pair helps to raise children, a cleaning lady helps with comfort, a consultant helps to improve a business and a CEO motivates others in growing and achieving results.

If you had a job and decided to change employment, enjoy that victory. If you had no job but you found one, sign the contract and celebrate. If you had to change the job because you could not stand it anymore, leave the old employment even if the things are blooming. Leave even when your employer least expects it. Leave because you will always know that you did well. If the company needs you, it will get you back. In any circumstances leave an existing job while delivering results right up to the last day. Care about your work and stay smart and sharp until the last day of employment. Never wind down because you have dozens of other offers. Your commitment and dedication until the last day is the key ingredient to your professional pride. Regardless of where you are and how many other offers you have for future employment, stay committed to the existing job. It will never undermine your career ethics to remain responsible until the last working day.

Lesson 15: Always think of any job as a means to your self-development. If you have no job, get one – any place is a good place to start. If you have a job but you know that your investment is not appreciated, do not wait for someone to fill the last drop in your glass. Leave. Leave even when things are good and leave gracefully. Leave when you are at your best.

The Sightseeing

Studying and learning your inner abilities.

In the early stage of my professional journey, getting a good job was always a difficult process. I had to compete with other smart people and I always experienced moments that reminded me that I was a foreigner, even after living in Denmark for years. As a student, I invested hours of interview preparation, tons of online tests and quizzes and multiple personality tests. Preparation was a key for any interview I had. I was sharp at my interviews and I was well-prepared. I was a dedicated, hard-working candidate but at times I received comments about my language skills. I studied day and night for seven years in Denmark, not just improving my language skills but developing my entire personality and behaviour. After years of constant self-development and self-awareness work, I needed to be taken more seriously. My language skills played a minor part in who I was as a candidate.

Lesson 16: When you are in a process of establishing yourself, think big, think options and think smart. Don't let others ruin or even undermine your confidence. Trust yourself regardless of what others say.

Many interviews I attended were quite good and several times I made it to the top three candidates. In the end, someone else was chosen and I had to look further. I was not losing belief in myself but I started doubting how long it would take for me to find a job. With time I became more indifferent and I began to slowly question the skills that I had. Thinking and analysing too many interviews, hoping to find my inner true abilities as an employee, I discovered a much more powerful skill. The skill of daring to reach impossible goals.

Once I went for a run near a beach on a cold November day. I didn't have a job at that time and I needed to fuel my emotional well-being. During that run, I was tempted by a thought that one day I would be able to swim outside during the winter. It was an idea for literally a few seconds and the cold temperature emphasised that it could never happen. And I guess I didn't dare. Many days went by and I still could not switch off my thinking about the jobless situation. I had to do something different to change my attention and to ease my worries. Many weeks went by after my first vague idea about winter swimming. I left for my usual run one day and decided to check how cold the water was. I was not ready to stand up to the challenge. I just had to try something new and something difficult. I didn't even know if I would get horribly sick after a cold swim but it was not my priority. Trying something outside of any comfort zone was more important. I finished my run, took off everything but my bikini, went in the water and got enormous chills immediately. I could barely spend a few seconds in the water. My toes started to become numb. I ran back to my car, drove home and took a long hot shower to get my normal temperature back. I didn't get sick. Instead, I was intrigued by what I had experienced.

From that day, I continued with the cold-water routine until the end of December. I finally took my first real swim in freezing cold water several days before Christmas. It was cold but I felt like I had just won a million dollars. More than a million. I had achieved something many people would think was impossible. I was back into my shoes and I felt the world was at my feet. I found a way to overcome my jobless situation by simply finding another goal and focusing on that goal. My goal was not just to try winter swimming but to push my limits and discover my skills. Eventually, I understood that the impossible is possible. I found a great job and I was at the top of my well-being and health.

Lesson 17: Always find new goals, small or big. No matter the context or purpose, have a goal and stick to it. If it is hard to have a goal, find a hobby that will make you motivated. If you cannot, introduce the word must in your life – something that will drag you off the couch and make you proud of what you can achieve on your own.

I achieved a lot with winter swimming. I still practice it. From one time a week, I eventually went swimming every day during the winter. It took many years of training, reading and mental preparation. I gradually increased the number of minutes I could spend in the cold water and decided to keep increasing my personal record. From a few seconds, I raised the bar to several minutes. Who knows what I'll be able to do in the future? I believe that there is no limit to our perfection and we can always keep on exploring the ambition we have.

To have goals and ambitions, to believe and trust in yourself is a never-ending story. While working towards new ambitions, remember to take a break and check-in with yourself. Because the minute you realise that the search for an ambition is fading away, you risk losing your biggest power: the power of life and our presence. If such a loss happens, think like a child. Think that there are many things left to be discovered. Think that there are very many unachieved aims in front of us – seas and oceans of opportunities. I am personally looking forward to finding new ambitions. To living those ambitions and to enjoying them. Most importantly, I am looking forward to the beauty of living my life and trusting in my inner power and the things that I can achieve simply by daring. I embrace the feeling of being alive in all the bits and pieces of my body. I savour love and hate, anxiety and happiness, frustration and completeness. I will never question myself anymore, why I needed to compete with others in finding a job. I will just compete. And I will never give up.

The Danger

It is OK to acknowledge weakness.

I am not a perfect person. None of us are. We often are at our best. But at times, we overestimate how much we can handle. We might lose track of what we need and what we really live for. It is wired that we hardly learn from other's mistakes. We need to go through all the experiences ourselves to understand the stupidity of our own actions. We overload our own capacity and forget to acknowledge that it is never too late to catch a moment and to offload the burden from our shoulders.

I have always been an achiever who needed a goal. I was not looking for perfection in everything; I just wanted to live a fulfilled life with ambitions, desires, wishes and victories. After I gave up my Belarusian citizenship to become a Dane because I wanted to settle in Denmark, I lost the passion for all of my ambitions. I had opportunities laying at my feet and I did not enjoy it. It was such a strange feeling. I did not know what to fight for and what to live for. I lost track of my everyday small wishes, big ambitions and future achievements. My core happy life recipe was flying away from me as if it never existed. I had my own apartment, my own cool car, a great job and an amazing boyfriend. Yet something was wrong. My mind suddenly turned old, moody and weak. My behaviour was confusing to me. There were days I did not know my own mind. I would function well during the day as if nothing was different. Yet the feeling that a strong and wise girl was turning into a mess of confusion and frustration was growing stronger each day.

Lesson 18: When you feel you are about to hit a wall, have a good talk with a dearest friend, your family or a professional therapist. Or even a light friendly conversation with a stranger in the street can help you to get a simple emotional relief. Because by talking, we get our feelings out of our bodies. Never ignore the discomfort in your head. It will never do any good. React and don't let the frustration keep drifting away. Don't assume that this is just another bad day. Wake up and do something about it.

My first hint about my deep enormous emotional trouble was a video that was recorded by mistake. It was horrible. I was crying my heart out looking at a picture of my mother. I was miserable. Many years had gone by since my mother's death and it took me many years to realise what I was going through. I was hiding my sorrow for a long time. And I was alone. Only when I became a mother myself, did I finally understand what an enormous connection a mother and child share. Becoming a mother was the missing element that I needed to let go of the pain of losing my mom – my one and only true love and the only very deep connection to a dearest person. It literally took me almost 20 years to finally cry out all tears and put the loss of unlimited love behind me. The loss of the woman that gave me a life. The one that I never got a real chance to share my worries and achievements with, my love stories and my victories. The loss of a person who would always love me, no matter what, for those 20 years. The one, who I remembered was holding my hand on a cold winter evening, walking to a store to buy candy for New Year's Eve. I could not feel the cold that evening. All I remember was walking together with my mother feeling happy and warm.

Lesson 19: Even if you are the strongest person on the planet, cry and feel sorrow for your losses. Be weak, even if you don't want others to see it. Release the pain, even if it means appearing weak and tired. Do not hide your feelings. Be fragile and be sad. For a moment, for minutes, for days or even months. Just not for a lifetime.

My mother was a tough lady. She never spoke to us about the deep topics of life or the essence of the human existence. She was a very busy woman raising eight of us. She was a strict mom and I was a little troublemaker. When she passed away, after just a few weeks in a hospital bed, all I could think of on the day of the funeral was that I wanted the whole farewell ritual to end as soon as possible. The body of my mom was in a coffin in the middle of our house. By local traditions at that time, the body of my mother needed to stay in our house, so both my mom's soul and my family could say a proper farewell. I was not ready to say goodbye and I was running away from reality. So I went to my bedroom and I fell asleep in the middle of the day, while family and friends came to say goodbye to my mother. When I woke up, I was happy to realise that it was a time to take my mom to the cemetery and in a few minutes the whole thing would be over. I saw many crying faces in our house. I could not stand the sad aura of the funeral. I didn't want to be a part of it and I was trying to escape as much as I could from that reality. In the end, I saw my mother's face before the coffin was closed but I never said a proper goodbye to her as in the Russian tradition.

Only 20 years later could I release my pain, after years of emotional turmoil and many tears that no one could see. There was a warm evening in the spring of 2015. I sat on the balcony of my apartment and suddenly I heard a bird. It was singing so nicely that I was absolutely taken by its voice. In my thoughts, I started chatting with that bird, asking how things were and if the bird was doing fine. The small little bird was singing sweetly. I felt great and my heart was at peace. In a matter of seconds, I realised that the bird was my mom's soul. And exactly at the very second I thought of it, the bird spread the wings and flew by me very gracefully. I concluded that it was indeed the spirit of my mother and I went to bed. 20 years had gone by and I finally closed the loss of my mother in my heart.

Lesson 20: With that experience, I realised that all I needed to get back into normal shape was love. Indefinite and unconditional love.

Even if it sounds crazy, that silent chat with a bird, that quiet moment of release showed me that I had found myself again by letting the loss of my mom rest forever. I did it quite late and I carried the pain with me for a long time without knowing or realising it. Don't wait if you ever end up in a place I was. Be smarter than me. Sort out your thoughts and emotions and let them rest forever. If you need to take some days off, do so; cut contact with your friends and even family so you can be alone. No one will judge you for that. And if someone does, remember that the only way to stand firmly on your feet is the power of finding your strong feet when hope is lost. You'll find the power to search a way out of a deep forest by feeling the strength in your legs as you walk the miles to find the exit you desire.

The Escape

Don't rush.

The moment of relief connected to my mother's death raised a lot of thinking about myself, my life and what I desired. I did very well with all my small victories and I was hungry for life. Ever since I'd moved to Denmark, my life was fast-paced and I was constantly on the run. I have and I will cherish all the achievements and all the great life lessons I had. The fast highway speed of my life adventures was the secret magic to who I am today and what I am capable of. The speed of all events taught me that if I ever lose a sense of a direction, a time or a day, I can immediately remind myself that all my worries are only within me.

Living at a fast-pace and building my life from scratch in Denmark was – and still is – great. My many years in Denmark were so dynamic and fun that I gained enormous self-confidence as I had more fun with colourful living. I was rarely stressed out. I liked doing many things at once and I enjoyed the variety of my days and my life experiences. As I was raising my daughter on my own, I found I could manage everything myself. Everything except how tired I was. One day I woke up and started the normal routine, cuddling, breakfast, clothes on, in the car and off to my daughter's day-care. I didn't realise until we were standing outside the day-care with the lights off that it was Sunday.

Lesson 21: When things are too much to bear, you don't owe anything to anyone apart from yourself. Don't call and don't meet with friends if you don't want to. Don't do dishes if all you need is to sleep. Don't be nice to anyone apart from yourself. Be arrogant and cut the unnecessary loose talk. Focus on yourself.

After many years of living at a fast pace, working hard and keeping many commitments, I realised that I did not have to rush to my successes at the speed of light and I do not need to do as many things as I did before. I did not need to write long text messages to my friends explaining why I could not come to birthday parties, nor did I need to show up for a coffee appointment if I had not slept well. I did not need to be nice to all the people I knew. And I didn't need to be a support shoulder for many friends anymore. The shoulder was weak and it needed to be healed. I realised that there were only two people I had to care about and to be nice to and they were my daughter and myself. I did not choose to be selfish to my friends. I simply had no energy or desire to race through life anymore. I needed some peace. And I needed a good night's sleep.

I sat down and I created a map of my life and my surroundings at that time. In the middle of the map, I had myself as a focal point. I added five or six circles around me – my family, my friends, my work, etc. Then I wrote down three bullet points in each of those circles highlighting the things that were bothering me. All of them appeared to contain some factor of emotional exhaustion. While doing this mapping of worries, I was amazed by the fact that all I needed was to write down keywords. They were so obvious that I did not need to explain or elaborate on their meaning. I ended up outlining my pain points and when I was done, I already felt a little bit easier.

Lesson 22: Do the homework of cleansing your brain. Start doing it on your own. Write down all that bothers you. Look at it but don't solve the puzzle yet. You have been inside of your brain so much that you won't find the answers immediately. Solve this homework outside of your own settings. This is a perfect time to get an outside view, a professional expert, a close family or a friend.

I shared my map with a professional psychologist and we had great conversations about many parts of those circles that I had sketched. Many conversations, months of conversations. We have spent a good long time on it. With the speed of a turtle, I started cleaning up the mess in my head. Things began to function for me again and I felt that I needed to cut some things from my mind. I needed to read just the way I functioned and I had to drastically rearrange some of the vital elements in my everyday life. I initiated a few life-changing routines and started by looking at my lifestyle and my everyday routine. My text messages became simpler with no long explanations, long sentences or perfect grammar rules. My talks on the phone became concrete and short. I focused on what I needed to hear and not what was nice to chat about. I became very direct with all the friends and family I talked to. And sometimes, maybe, too direct to the point of being rude by modern measures. The bottom line was that it was a conscious tactic for me to get my mental and physical form back to the bikini shape. I stopped small chats on the phone and I don't even miss them today. What I missed was not a telephone chat; it was face to face deep conversations that gave and will always give me enormous satisfaction. Just like sessions I had with my therapist with natural, sincere, old-fashioned and real-life conversations. Nothing can replace human communication. With the emotional release came the physical clean up, I stopped excusing myself that my body was not back to its pre-birth weight. I started losing it. I started thinking of new ways of re-energising my body and I went on a full detox.

The Repair

Detox both your body and mind.

That Sunday morning when I stood in front of the closed day-care with my daughter, I was exhausted. I could not get enough sleep. I was a worn-out human that needed some serious detox – a cleansing of my mind, my body and emotional exhaustion. The time, of course, was one element of my tiredness. I had gone for almost three years as a single mom, caring for my baby alone, not having a family around me to support. I tried to balance my work and private life but I literally had no time for myself. I knew it and I realised it. Those were the consequences of my own decision to be a single mom. But it was not the reason why I was so tired. My daughter created an enormous euphoria and gave me a brand-new perspective on life. I had taken on a huge responsibility and I knew that with such responsibility, the consequences were incvitable. It was OK that I lacked sleep and it was fine that I forgot what it was like to have uninterrupted sleep. Forgot for years.

Being a single mom was not the primary reason for my exhaustion. Although, of course, it did play a role. But the real reason for my exhausted body was the fact that both my body and my mind needed a cure and some good care because I raced around like a crazy car, though the jungles of ambitions, battles, challenges and my independence for decades. I had run so fast to get a good education, fancy career and a brand-new life in a foreign country that I only allowed myself short breaks. I rarely stopped and caught my breath before I looked for a new challenge. I am not complaining, nor do I regret it. If I could live my life experiences again, I would choose to have the same hunger for a better life, success and development that I have experienced so far. I would have the same ambitions, same drive and go at the same speed. The only thing that I would reconsider is the number of stops I would make during the journey toward my successes.

The reason for my tiredness was the speed of my life makeover and the speed of my self-development. Becoming a mom that turns values and perspectives upside down and relieving the pain of losing my biological mother gave me the last hint of what I needed. I had to start listening to myself and being wise about taking time off. Small breaks were needed for me to regain emotional stability and a complete detox to energise my body. In a nutshell, I needed to treat my body and mind well to slow down the speed of exhaustion.

Lesson 23: Always remember that your body and mind can adjust to any circumstances. It is just a matter of time. But when you catch yourself thinking that all you have achieved means nothing, take it seriously and go on a detox.

So I detoxed. I went for all beauty treatments that I could allow myself and to all the medical exams that I needed. I browsed the internet to get tips on healthy foods and healthy living. I continued healing my mind with my therapist and I filtered out the unwanted noise from my brain. I found the time in the morning to cuddle with my baby girl instead of rushing out of bed and counting minutes before we had to be in the car ready to go. I accepted that she cried at the most inconvenient times in the mornings. When she did, I would sit down on the same level with her and hug and kiss her, even if I had only five minutes to get ready afterward.

From my childhood, I recall that I was a very energetic girl but also a very lazy one at times. I liked playing for hours and I also liked chilling in front of the television. That childish chill time contributed to the way I worked on detoxing my body and mind. I have not just lived on fresh juices every day during the detox; I combined it with good sleep, exercise and primitive detox medicine that could literally clean my body from things stored for ages. I started taking vitamins to get my energy up, together with the cleansing medicine and regular cold swimming. I went shopping to renew my wardrobe. I started creating a filter in my head, that slowly began to sort out the worries from my mind so they would not end up in my analysis box. I had to cut out unnecessary information that created noise in my head and I avoided meeting certain individuals to detox my surroundings.

Lesson 24: There is nothing wrong with giving yourself some slack and spending a day doing nothing. No one can function day and night pretending to be a perfect person full of energy. We all need space and time away from regular things, so let yourself be lazy.

I detoxed the level of my professional growth by changing to a company where I could still grow but where my family could not be the number one priority. I detoxed my family worries and cut contact with some family members. I was not cruel or impolite; some of my family members looked at the values I had differently and I did not need an extra layer of stress in my head just because it was a family member's expectation I was dealing with. Family or not, it was important for me to create and customise my settings. When a person is tired and cannot see clearly anymore, it's dangerous to sacrifice sanity, to be nice to the family or friends around.

I finally cleared my old clothes from my closet and I sent them to charity. In the process of clearing out my closet, I realised that I was cleaning my mind. I visualise the things that I really needed and I gave away the things that were secondary and simply nice to have. I took away unnecessary stuff and left the simple, minimalistic items that I really needed. There was still ten percent of the work left but I was happy with the result. There will always be that five or ten percent imperfection in our daily lives but I learned to relax about it. What I kept unchanged in my wardrobe was the number of shoes I had. I love shoes. I believe all women do. But for me, that was the only element that I did not need to change. Shoes give me colour in my busy life. Colour. Colour is what gave me the grand culmination of the detox process. And that's why I decided that no matter how busy or tired I can be, I would always wear a piece of colour every day; be it shoes, earrings, belts or another accessory.

Lesson 25: Don't underestimate the power of colour. Colours can reflect the state of your mind – the longing for a sunny day or happy moments. If you cannot see the light, even if you still see the sun in all its colours, detox. Detox your body and mind until you find your own cure and your own unique never-changing wardrobe item.

I believe that I am a fairly active person. I believe I've achieved a lot. That said, I still want to achieve more. But I managed to learn how to get loose, lie on a couch pretending to watch TV and browse channels even if I have no interest in watching TV at all. I have learned to create my free zone with the purpose of no meaning. No meaning for hours, minutes and seconds. I learned how to park the chase for finding meaning in all I did, at least for a short time. We all need time to switch off our minds, even if it feels like the time is somewhat wasted, to help our brains relax, sort out any unnecessary information overload and cut the garbage that has been stored for days or even months. Or even years. Yoga, meditation and very good sleep are the perfect alternatives to meaningless TV watching. I did try all of them apart from meditation, real meditation. I am not practicing this very tempting skill yet because I want to meditate correctly. To learn meditation, I need more free time and I need to be well, not to jeopardise my mental well-being. So real meditation is something that is always on my list of new discoveries and I am looking forward to mastering it one day. No matter the tool that I can use to relax, the final desired product is less noise and more balance in my life. And now also my little daughter's life.

Lesson 26: When you get lazy, enjoy the time but remember to not stop caring about the way you look and the way you feel. Never stop caring for yourself under any circumstances. I would take my favourite high heels to the moon, so I can sing and dance looking great and feeling content after my lazy break.

Get a full detox, consisting of a functional daily routine for yourself, a cleansing of your body and a full awareness of your feelings. As a result of a full-scale detox, you can easily get into your car in the morning and start explaining to your car how good you feel today. Perhaps, a weird way of releasing emotions but by speaking out loud, no matter whether it is in a car, your home or any other private place, the fact still remains that our tensions get out much more quickly from our bodies. The release of emotions is immediately out in space when we talk about them. Find some unique place to speak up, a place you can hear yourself and you feel comfortable. My place is nature. I take a run; I sing while running, not being afraid that someone will hear me and I feel great. The combination of fresh air, cold water swimming and my alone time gives me a kick and keeps me alive in a full detox process. Doing that, I get many ideas on how to lift my ambitions to a higher level and I realise how good it is to offload burdens and any heaviness that I have carried inside of me for ages. Enjoy your full detox, I am sure you will be on the top of your wellbeing and feel fantastic.

The Fuel

Night dreams shape the mind toward superior beliefs.

I dream a lot. I dream every night. I have read tons of books about my dreams and I have not found a concrete answer about their meaning. Knowing myself and my never-give-up nature, I had to come up with my own interpretation. Every morning I woke up, I remembered not just one dream but many. I had to know their meaning. Dreams are obviously connected to our feelings and emotions, so the interpretation, I came up with, was that the dreams were my secret desires and a fine digestion of all my daily feelings and impulses. We repress a lot of emotions during the day and try to disguise many true impulses. During the night we digest those feelings with no control, no power over our own conscious images. Knowing how to digest hidden emotions is an enormous skill that eventually allows us to wake up in the morning fresh and happy, even if we felt miserable the day before.

In earlier chapters, I mentioned that I love my job and I appreciate the steep career lessons that I have had and continue to have. My passion to improve, learn and work on self-development will never be exhausted. I will keep on using my drive and willingness to make a difference until I am very old. Therefore, my character and my personality are not a perfect fit for any company and I have to be very careful in selecting a job. There was a job that I knew was not a perfect match but I chose the company because I knew that I could contribute and I had a perfect bond with the team and many of the colleagues I was working with. I was proud of my work and I was promised benefits, new tasks and more responsibility. After months of effort, I did not get anything and I questioned whether I was really capable of making a difference for the firm. I kept on thinking and one day I left work, extremely frustrated and I had used almost the entire day just thinking about work. Before I fell asleep that day, I had several explanations in my head about why and how things were not working out. The dream I had that night cleaned up my worries in a snap of the fingers. I woke up early the day after, feeling fresh and happily alive and I even had time to cuddle with my daughter. I felt on the top of the world.

In my dream that night, I was playing with a girl my age. I believe she was either my soul mate or a very close friend. We were both running around a big house with many rooms playing and laughing. The girl said that it was time to fly out of a window. We opened a window and I saw the night sky, the clouds bright like daylight, very peaceful and beautiful. I was scared to go out but my trust in that girl who was holding my hands was much stronger. I took her hand and we flew out that window. We started flying around, smiled at each other and kept on holding hands. We flew up and down in the clouds, twisting and turning. I repeated each move after that girl and I was very happy. We started laughing eventually. We could not see each other's faces up in the clouds but kept holding on to each other and our every move was synchronised. We had so much fun together that I felt comfortable, light and not scared of the open spaces around us. We flew back into the house through the same window and continued laughing.

Coming home from work, I had felt frustrated and could not stop thinking about the reasons my hard work and best efforts for the company were not recognised. After my night's digestion, I woke up and understood that the heavy clouds at work are the worries that I'd had for months but the content of the dream meant I had trust in myself and my abilities. That dream meant that I knew who I was, as an employee and I was not afraid of taking risky decisions. That is why I was flying high in my dream, feeling happy and at ease. That girl that I was playing with in my dream was my reflection and she showed me who I really was. I was a happy person and committed employee because I laughed so much in my dream and I trusted the way my reflection girl was leading me. I was a happy girl with full of confidence in what to do because I could fly freely in the open sky and I could twist and turn the way I wanted not falling down. I was the girl who enjoyed every cloud in the sky because I didn't let go of the hands of my reflection-girl.

I have had other powerful, scary and strange dreams and some of the dreams I have managed to write down when the time allowed. I knew that it was very important to just write inconsistent sentences the minute I woke up. Dreams have no logic and are very confusing but that's exactly what I was trying to write down, the illogical sentences and meaningless words. The first dream that I tried to record made almost no sense to me. That is because I was not focusing on the dream itself but on making the dream, have logical connections and meaning. After writing down many dreams, I could finally see that it was not about connecting the uncompleted sentences that I wrote down the minute I woke up; it was all about my emotions.

Lesson 27: Try to write down your dreams. Just writing the keywords is sufficient. Write inconsistent sentences if you have multiple dreams in one night. Do not try to find logic. Do not try to express or conclude immediately on what you have dreamed about. Leave the notes for some time. Never start interpreting the dreams on the same day. Give it some time. Come back and read the notes after a few days. You will be amazed by how much sense they make.

Dreams give us strength and they deepen our worries, depending on where we are in our lives. They promote grand emotions. They are an obvious definition, a symbol that your wishes and desires are what you want to achieve, no matter what it takes. Once I was coming out of full anaesthesia after an operation and almost fought with the nurse so she would not wake me up. I was playing with my daughter in my dream that happened just a few minutes before the nurse started waking me up. I was so occupied by taking care of my daughter who needed my attention in my dream, that's all I could focus on was my baby girl. No one could stop me from taking care of her. I had to wake up and I did.

My first emotion, the second the nurse woke me up was the fear of being separated from my daughter. That's perhaps the biggest fear I have even today. I started crying. I was so miserable that even the doctors did not understand what was happening. I kept on saying that I needed to take care of my daughter. I did not choose to cry but my tears were uncontrollable. Only after some time when I had calmed down, I realised that becoming a mom and bringing a huge responsibility into this world meant everything to me. It was not just a side effect of the anaesthesia. That strange awakening dream meant that I will always carry a worry in my heart. The worry that one day my daughter and I will get separated. But that dream also meant that she will always be priority number one, no matter what condition I am in. I will hold my grip like a bulldog till the last moment to protect her.

Dreams also give us magnificent ideas and inner inspiration. Lots of inspiration. Some of the dreams I had were cruel and scary. I would dream that I had a chain around me and I could not escape and be free. Scary to the point that I would be awake during the night, lying in my bed and wondering what I had done wrong. Lying awake for several hours, I would contemplate and think before I could fall asleep again. I've had plenty of cruel and unpleasant dreams. At the time, I thought they meant that something bad was going to happen to me. But after many years, I understood that in real life, they meant the opposite. The scary and horrible dreams I had meant that I was dealing with real worries in my daily life. And only the scary dreams could take my worries go away as if all the worries I just had a night before would vanish in the morning. As if my mind was going through some cleansing process during the night so that in the morning, I would wake up ready to live another day knowing what to do and knowing what was bothering me.

Being an optimist, I have always believed that there is a solution for everything and that some night dreams can turn into fantasy. I had an excellent dream in 2015. The dream meant the projection of my future life based on some fantasies generated through the years. I knew the meaning of that dream but I didn't know if it would come true or not. We are unable to turn our dreams into real-life happenings and fairy tale situations, just as we want them to be. But what all of us are capable of is turning wishes into real-life dreams. Of course, night dreams cannot be rebuilt into reality. The perfect match between the night and a real-life dream cannot be found and maybe the match should never be found at all. If we look at what is really hidden behind our secret wishes and magnificent dreams during the night, then it's quite easy to see that the night dreams trigger our inner beliefs about a great future. And these beliefs initiate an amazing process of building something extraordinary instead of reproducing the night dream content.

Lesson 28: You don't need to rebuild your night dreams and you don't need to know the concrete meaning behind your dreams. Transform the night dreams into a powerful, real, present, everyday dream. A real-live dream can become much more exciting than the night fantasy.

That dream I had in October 2015 showed me what I was looking forward to establishing, whether it came true or not. It was a hint of what I was trying to build from scratch. And it was a reminder for me to enjoy every moment of the dream and the process of reaching that dream ambition. I don't know how I will get closer to achieving that dream but I know that I will do whatever it takes to realise that missing element. I know that because when I woke up that morning, I felt that I wanted to close my eyes and keep on seeing that dream forever.

Any good person gets a reward and unexpected life surprises, sooner or later. Of course, it will almost always happen when we least expect it. But it happens to all of us. It happened to me. I gave up the idea of marriage a long time ago and I had no wishes to marry at all. Many of my friends do not understand that. They cannot understand why marriage is not important to me when I say that I do not believe in marriage. And maybe, more importantly, I don't dream about marriage, neither at night nor during the day. I believe in love. Love that can have many faces and shapes and love that can last forever. We do not have to get married just because others do that. But we can fall in love with a person with not being together. And we can love any person unconditionally, cherish and develop that feeling of love for a lifetime. My deepest value is that love is a long and magical journey. We do not fall in love at first sight. The first sight is a great excitement and passionate feeling. Anyone can and should experience that. True and long-lasting love is a process and it's the most wonderful experience one can ever have. Long-lasting love is not a night dream for me. It's real and it's present every day.

The Engine

When love goes away, try to let it go.

True and long-lasting love is extraordinary. It is also weird and confusing at times. We just have to be in love and we can cross many hurdles and obstacles, unrealistic barriers and mountains. It is a magically unexplained cure against many diseases and pains – a medicine that saves the world and stops wars that, in fact, start because we all defend the people and values around us. I have two sisters, both tried marriage and ended up divorced. My oldest sister was actually married and divorced twice with the same guy. It was a very strange family situation but I have never judged my sister. She had enough judgment from my family. I talked to my sister, trying to understand what happened. She said that she was not in love anymore and I wondered how was that possible. She had beautiful kids, a good husband, a big house and working relationships. It was so hard for me to understand my sister and why she couldn't find a way to save her family. Most importantly, I could not figure out why she didn't try to save the many years of love that made her want to establish the family in the first place.

During my student times in Denmark, I met many great international people from different places and countries.

There was one particular classmate who I remember was quite a character and had a great personality. Almost the whole school knew him and he was absolutely fantastic. He had so many sparks in him that it was energising just talking to him. We dated for three months and only then did I agree to become his girlfriend. I needed the time to feel love and, of course, I did love that amazing person. Deeply and utterly. It was the type of love that lifted me up and made me stronger. We spent six years together and we even got engaged. The last year of our relationship turned into a mess of conflicts and we fought for things that had no value and no meaning. I kept asking myself why this got so bad and why we could not just get married and have beautiful kids together. My heart was hurting but, in the end, I found the answer. After so many years together, I stopped believing in a story with a happy ending. We lifted each other up in the first few years; we balanced each other for the next two or three years and we lost our connection in the years after. We stopped seeing each other's values and the feeling of love started disappearing after five or six years together. After the years of emotional struggle, we lost each other. That unconditional love for each other from the day we met could not cure our wounds and could not fix our problems. The scary part was realising that in the end, I had no wish or desire to work the things out. The only exit I saw was to let this great person go, so he could find another love who could give him the warmth and care that he needed and deserved.

Lesson 29: We all wish that love would last forever. I truly hope the wish comes true for you. Many of us, however, know that love might fade away sooner or later. When this happens, let go of your love and give that love a chance to find another home. Letting go is a form of love. The love that you held for many years deserves freedom and a chance to open the doors for other great love opportunities.

I grew up in a big family and I rarely hugged or kissed my parents or my siblings. But I knew that they needed me and they loved me no matter what. Family love. I retained so much of the unused love during my childhood that my reserves of love are enormous today. Therefore, I love so many people in my heart. My love has many forms and many types. No matter the type of love I have, it can last for a lifetime or it can last for just a few moments. I have experienced many types of love. Only lately, I finally discovered unconditional love. Not only because I became a mother and love my daughter unconditionally but because there are many other people that I love deeply and I will always love them for the rest of my days. Some of them I have only met recently and some of them are my family and long-time friends. I have developed a life-long commitment for each of them during very particular events and situations. Unconditional family love came very late to me, most likely during the birth of my daughter when I finally understood what family means. I did not realise that I love my sisters and brothers, my parents, my close friends and many other dear people unconditionally before that. Better late than never.

Just as we all love many people; we all have our own unique interpretations of love's limits and boundaries. We all have them but many of us are not aware of those boundaries. It took me some time to understand that I have only one simple love limitation: loving where I am not needed. The feeling of not being needed by anyone can destroy our lives. When we feel not needed, we fade away. Why be in love with a person who clearly does not need me and the love has no place to go? I have experienced one-sided love. My best explanation as to why I was holding on to the one-way love was that I tried to build a fantasy, escape from reality and hide behind the feeling of love. It was not an easy process for me to just stop being in love when I knew that I was not needed. I had to find a way of dealing with one-sided love. I looked for a solution to that and I found it. I found the way to live with a love that was just in me. The hint of how to establish that not needed love boundary came in a dream after long and heavy contemplation about why love needs to have limitations.

One day I woke up scared because I could not fly in my dream. I had a dream that I was a bird and I was ready to spread my wings and fly around. I took off but then I saw that the sky was turning into a wooden ceiling. There was no blue sky. There was no fresh air. There was wood everywhere. On the wall, the ceiling, the floor. I was caught in a wooden box with no way to escape. All was closed. I could not get out. I was trapped and I wanted to fly away. I was trapped and I could hardly breathe. I was locked up and I was afraid. I woke up and I had to promise myself that I would cherish any unconditional love because it made me alive and made me feel my heart. But it was a time to put my feelings aside from that unconditional one-sided love. It was not a decision to forget the unconditional love feeling, nor was it about throwing images away and tearing the pictures apart that reminded me of that love. It was about a delicate choice to place the love into a room in my heart for anyone, so I would not go back to feeling unwanted and not needed. I wrote a goodbye note in my diary to close my thoughts and I stopped wondering why the love I had could not become real.

Lesson 30: The cure against many dead-end situations is rooted in your personal boundaries. Search, find and establish them. A love boundary is just one example of why we need to establish borders, be kind to ourselves and keep on flying freely in the open blue sky.

I thought that one-sided love was a waste of my feelings when I was writing a goodbye note and I was sure that this was the correct explanation. But I was wrong. Many years after that dream of flying freely, I came back to the unwanted love again and I replaced that love with an almost unconditional one again. It felt as if the love feeling came back to me in another way and another form.

Long or short, love is good. Love is healthy even unconditional, one-sided love. Love means you are alive and you have feelings. You don't simply exist on the planet but you live a pleasant life and the heart that is resting in your body is warm. Love is natural medicine. Love your children, parents, flowers, animals, sun, water and cars. Become a love addict. And when a love boundary needs to be established, enjoy the power of free-flying and fresh air, have a break and place the love in a secret corner. Just don't forget about it. It might come back.

The Gearshift

Being a single mom is the greatest privilege and pride.

Growing up as a teenager, I dreamed that a prince would find me, just like many other girls did. I dreamed there would be the one and only man that I would love and cherish for the rest of my days. I had the same dreams as many girls and I believed in a standard parenting model, just like the one I was raised in, having both parents and many siblings. The minute I found out that I was pregnant twisted the whole world upside down. The teenage dream of a prince disappeared and I ended up in a situation that I would never imagine being in because I knew that I was facing a single parent life from day one. I was scared. I didn't know the consequences and I was certainly not prepared. Knowing my ability to manage tough life situations, I knew that I had the strength to accept another challenge, especially this one. However, I was not ready or prepared but I wanted to go through a completely new life chapter with all the responsibility and an unknown future.

The happily-ever-after dream was not a choice anymore and I shifted to a modern family relationship model. It was modern because both parents jointly decided to have a child but the standard family living, joint commitment and shared responsibilities were not part of the deal. The excitement about the project was big and both parents were equally happy to bring about a new life, even though they were not in a standard relationship. The best part was that my daughter's father supported our common decision to become contemporary, which is very unusual to many other families' situation. I, of course, knew that my future was not exactly what I had dreamed of. But at that time, I didn't matter. I was happy that my daughter had her father around and I was looking forward to raising a child in a modern relationship. What I didn't know was that agreeing to a modern family model literally meant a single-parent life. I hoped that the joint decision in the early stage of my pregnancy meant shared responsibility in the long run. That hope had vanished with time and I was left alone on a 24/7 shift. Every day and every night. I had no family that I could ask for help when I needed it badly. I had only a few friends who could respond immediately. I was alone. But some inner power inside of me and my ability to fight for my daughter's life and for mine made me believe that no matter what, I would manage.

Lesson 31: Blessing comes rarely and very unexpectedly. When it comes and with riches for you, accept and make the most of it. Even if you are not ready, take the risk to accept the unknown. There is no readiness formula for many life situations but there are always your strengths. Believe in yourself, even if no one believes in you and enjoy the amazing outcome you build on your own.

My daughter was indeed a blessing. She was not the exact dream I had. She was much better than the life experience I was looking forward to. And she was the last missing bit of why I started writing about my life.

My biggest challenge and my biggest fear were about to arrive, which meant, among other things, the ultimate never-changing love. The pregnancy went great. I went to all the doctor's appointments alone. I ensured that I ate well and exercised often. For seven months, I practiced swimming in cold water, carrying a baby girl in my body. I bought baby things alone and I made sure that everything was ready in the house to meet a new member of the planet. Not having a handy helper around, I became a handy mom myself, assembling baby furniture and drilling holes in the walls while pregnant.

While waiting for the birth of my daughter, I was worried. Worried about many things that I could not share with anyone because I didn't even know what to ask. Many things were so unfamiliar to me. During some conversations, I was hearing remarks from others that being a single mom was a hard job and all I could think was that my mom gave birth to eight children, yet she remained a cheerful and strong woman. Hence, I knew that I could definitely handle one child. I did not like the single-mom pity conversations and I still do not like hearing the 'poor single mom' talks today. Single mothers are the strongest people I know. Single moms are not a charity case as some people think. Single moms are some of the best, most caring people of all time. They nurture new lives alone and they do a stunning job. I knew that I was prepared to meet my new lifestyle and I was prepared to deal with any obstacle along the way, alone.

My miracle was born and I started the race of sleepless nights, constant worries and 24/7 anxiety. But I survived. And

I managed well. It is very hard to describe how I managed; every day was tough and had many unforeseen situations but I kept carrying on. It took many months to stabilise the daily routine, find the rhythms, which was the same as it is for other parents. I was prepared for the daily work and the amount of focus that was needed. What I was not prepared for was far from material things and daily routine. I was not prepared emotionally. I had hard times dealing with the notion of being alone. I was scared during the nights, alone with a baby crying for hours nonstop. I could not sleep well for months because I needed to hear my baby breathe and I was alert every day worrying that something bad was going to happen. I needed support. I needed it badly. But I was alone.

Lesson 32: When you feel there is no one around to help and you are alone, find a way to get some sleep and carry on. Live even if your life runs on survival mode every day. Live. Find a way to face your fears and find a way to deal with them. Stay responsible. Cry in your pillow if you need to. Feel sorry for yourself but do something about it.

Time is an amazing thing. Time heals everything. Time changes us, our thinking and our worries. Time constantly gives us new perspectives and time heals our wounded strengths. Time gave me a chance to learn how to manage my new life, not over some days but over years of hard work. Time made me a confident mom and a strong parent. My sense of responsibility for my daughter, stubbornness to survive through the hard nights and willingness to remain myself while raising my baby on my own made me a responsible mom. I proved to myself that I could move mountains if I wanted to and I have learned that being a single mom is much better than being hurt or miserable in a standard family relationship. I have also learned that no one can replace a father figure for my daughter but not having that figure around, I could provide both a mom and dad environment for my child by being strict and tough yet caring and loving. It is a true blessing to live in a very modern relationship compared to just some years ago when women were punished for having children outside of a marriage. The fact that I became a single parent with all of the burdens on my shoulders reflects the lifetime value that the life of my child is superior to mine. I had a strong urge to adjust to unexpected life conditions and I am very proud of it. The classic family model was not my choice any longer and I gladly accepted the modern way.

Lesson 33: Every parent has one thing in common: Responsibility for a child. Married or not, in a relationship or not, a child deserves to have both parents. My daughter has both parents, even if only one is fighting for her daily well-being and it is fine. Life as a single mom is a privilege, joy, great pride and ultimate love. The love of any single parent is enough to provide a secure home and care for a child.

The Crossroad

Embrace your relationships and your family DNA.

We can use determination in life-long relationships to understand and study our families, friends and surroundings. It is so important to have ambitions, not only in our lives but also in the lives of our families and friends. We need determination because when it comes to learning and understanding personalities and human behaviour, we face a huge complex web of feelings and events. Understanding the dynamics of my own family was always tricky. During my childhood, I never understood why it was so easy to live in a big family as a kid and why, during my teenage years, it was so hard to be eight kids in our family. I never talked about deep topics with my parents and rarely talked to my sisters. My brothers were always my brothers, with whom I would not even think about talking about sad and happy things. When I left for Denmark, I ended up alone with plenty of time to study my family's DNA.

During the first years of living in Denmark, I would often catch myself thinking how much I missed my family. My unconditional love for my family was not obvious at that time and hence the biggest question I asked myself was, "What am I really missing?" I enjoyed my wins and victories in

Denmark, I was successful and I was drifting away from my home country and my relatives. I even doubted if I wanted to go back home during the summer vacation and I barely called my parents once a month. During my childhood, I never talked to my siblings about my secrets, I had a very closed mind, although I was very outspoken and I never told my family that I loved them. Coming to Denmark at the age of 23, I was already an established personality and I could hardly change my fundamental attitude towards family and yet suddenly I started saying that I missed them. I believe I wanted to catch up on the missed connection to my family first and I truly wanted to learn my family DNA to come closer to almost-forgotten past events.

As a result of these feelings, I went home to Minsk for the first time after living in Denmark for almost a year. My family had grown since I was a kid; from 8 siblings, we had become 11 when my father remarried; it was to a strong woman who came into our family after my mother died. She guided my dad in many life decisions and she helped to raise four of my brothers, the youngest of whom was only seven and myself. She loved my dad so much. I could barely understand how she could take such a heavy burden to marry a man who had eight children from a previous relationship. I gained three bonus siblings and with time I started treating them just like my biological family. I purchased small gifts for everyone when I came home from Denmark. Literally everyone, sisters and brothers, stepsisters and stepbrothers, their wives and husbands, their kids and my parents, of course. The gifts I brought were very simple, what I could afford on my au pair earnings. The value of the gifts was not important. The happiness of my family was everything. I created a new tradition of giving gifts and sharing family love during that first visit and I felt unexplainably good realising how much my family needed me and I needed them and how much love we have being such a big family.

Lesson 34: No matter how long it might take for you to understand relationships and family DNA, keep on learning. Keep on searching. The reward will be a life lesson that you will cherish until the end of your days.

It took me many years to fully understand who my sisters and brothers were and it took me almost 35 years to understand who my father was. I have a feeling that I will learn more about my family in the future and I am looking forward to it. Things that I learned about my dad just a few years ago made me change my whole perception of him – beyond the honourable and hard-working person I knew. I'd never known his lifelong challenge to provide the food to such a big family, his sacrifice to drop out of his education and his dream to become an officer. Every time I travelled back home from Denmark, I arranged something fun to unite my family and get closer to my relatives. One of the greatest events was a family dinner with my dad and my brothers. My sisters could not make it to the dinner. During that evening, I made a quiz and wrote down very personal questions for them. I wanted to hear answers, share our childhood experiences, laugh, be happy and hear sincere answers in a room where everyone could speak freely. During that evening I learned that I will always volunteer to be a family psychologist and my office will always be open.

Lesson 35: Always accept the good and bad sides that you might discover about your family. Cherish and nurture family dynamics, the vast variety of differences and the unexplainable yet amazing family DNA.

There were many discoveries that evening and some of them are meant to stay within our family. Some of them were unexpected and some of them were very funny. I understood why my family is so complex and has a very distinct DNA. Hearing my father's story about a long struggle while raising the eight of us was quite a story. My dad shared his ambition about becoming an officer before there were too many of us. His answer showed me who I am and where my ambitions come from. The life of our parents and the secrets that they might carry for decades can reveal a whole world for us.

I love you, Dad, and I am who I am today because of you and Mom.

The Turn

Believe in the lifetime value of love.

I was 14 and he was 19. It was at my sister's wedding. I saw a handsome man who made my teenage heart dance as it had never danced before. He was so handsome and clever. He came from a big city and I was a teenage country girl. I did not have too much to offer and I did not stand out from the crowd. I was a little girl and he was everything I wished for.

We ended up sitting and talking under the trees in a warm place in a Belarusian town. His voice and his presence were more than I could wish for. I was enchanted and I was taken away by his every move. The way he walked, the way he talked, the way he smiled. Everything about him was perfect. If not for the growing cold that night, I could have stayed listening to him forever. But we had to say goodbye. The next day I confessed to my aunt that I really liked that guy. This wise woman told me to dress up and go see him. So, there I was, a little girl hoping that if I see him, the whole universe will change. I put my best outfit on and I went to see him. Not to beg him to stay with me. I knew that was impossible. I knew already that living in two different distant countries was not going to work. I was hoping to get his address so I could at least write him letters.

Lesson 36: Your first love and first affection can predict your future story. Your first love is not just another life experience. It tells you who you saw when you were young and naive. But most importantly, it reveals values that you will never live without.

I got his address and photo. I still remember that smile when he saw me the day after the wedding. Only he can tell me what it meant. All I remember was that I walked back home with my aunt feeling happy, I was happier than ever. I had his address so I could keep in contact with that beautiful man and I was already developing feelings for him. Many days went by before I received his first letter. I read that letter again and again and I even shared it with my closest friend. I received more letters. The letters kept me going with the warm and fulfilled love that I dreamed of as a teenage girl. And as a teenage girl, I developed that first love listening to 'Oh, baby, it's a wild world' music that was foreign to me but has remained in me ever since.

Time went by and I do not remember what happened to the letters. I was young and he was far away. At some point, I gave up and the letters were lost in time. I think six years passed by. I was rolling with my life and I never expected to see him again. My life developed and I grew up. I was looking for another type of love. I started my career and there was almost no memory left of that first love that I used to cherish. There was nothing left until one day that changed it all. I was going to my friend's house. I thought it was going to be just another dinner with all our friends I knew. I still remember when the door opened, that big door that opened up and I saw a ghost. Behind that door, after almost six years, I saw that familiar face. That face I looked for years and almost forgot. That face that was so dear me. There he was. My first love. My first affection. My everything. I could barely stand on my feet. I could not speak or move. I was frozen.

Lesson 37: First love is what you least expect to feel in your veins. First love is strange and comes around when you are not prepared. You can go around thinking that first love is just a foolish notion. And you are most likely right. It is foolish. And yet it is an extraordinary lifetime feeling.

We only had two days together. Two days after six years. Two days is nothing but for me it was everything. I knew I had to say goodbye eventually and go back to my regular life. The train that took my love away was the worst train in my life. That day the sky broke into miserable, tiny drops. I stood at the train station platform, everyone was happy and I was in pain. He was going away and I did not know if I would ever see his face again. The train left but I ended up standing on the train platform for several minutes getting soaking wet. My tears were colliding with the raindrops. I could not stand the trains, stations and the rain for many years after that moment. All I wanted was for him to stay with me, hold me and calm me down. But he left. He left and I have never seen him since then. My life went on. I kept his pictures in my album and I looked back at it sometimes. I would wonder how he is and would cherish that grand teenage love deep in my heart. I would often ask my sister about him but she could not tell me anything. My life went on for 20 years.

The story almost died. I left for Denmark. My whole world twisted. I developed as a person and I became much stronger than the teenage girl I was when I knew him. I became a career woman who was hungry for success and self-development. I knew where I was going and I knew who I loved. Then one day in 2016, something happened that made me believe once again that the impossible is possible. I learned that if you keep on looking, you will always eventually find what you are looking for. If you sincerely hang on to the power of your dream, you might get rewarded one day.

I sincerely wanted to know if life was treating him well but I could not find any information about him. I didn't have his letters anymore and I only remembered his name. I kept looking for many years until the day I found him. I did not have any expectations and I was not dreaming of a movie-style comeback. I just really wanted to hear about his life and to know that he was well. And maybe that is why I found him. The man I loved for many years, deep in my teenage heart, was walking down the streets of Denmark 20 years later. I recognised him from the first second. I had found him. The man my teenage heart fell in love with. The minute I saw him walking toward me, I felt like I needed to pull my memories out of my mind and then put them back again. We talked for hours that evening. We had a 20-year gap to catch up on and we had to get used to each other's company. It turns out we both had quite a story to tell each other.

Lesson 38: That first love formed a great human being in me. I know today why I can fall in love and what love actually means for me. That first love created a strong place in my heart. Love means caring for eternity. And that first love showed me that I can fall in love caring unconditionally with no demands, no expectations, no distance and no limits.

The Discovery

To share is to live.

Sharing is an essential ingredient of wellbeing, a free way towards a good life and a unique component in building our own unique dream. Sharing our material possessions and divine emotions, sharing food and making sure others are not starving is important. Sharing our smile and making others happy, even if it only lasts for a few seconds, is an honourable gesture. Sharing with a good heart and sharing sincerely leads to many of our greatest achievements.

I remember a grey November morning when I was delivering my daughter to her day-care. It was an ordinary day and it was just like any of the other mornings in our girly lives. But that particular morning I placed my daughter in her day-care and the minute I exited the institution, I found myself smiling. I was so happy and I was so energetic. The magic to my happiness was simple. I shared my smile and good mood not only with my angel but with the other kids in that day-care. I talked to almost every child I met that morning. I talked to them, mentioning their names, their siblings, their parents. I treated each and every one of them as a personality. I was personal to those kids and I meant it from the bottom of my heart. I mentioned their very unique skills, I smiled and I hugged them. I briefly talked to their parents as well but my focus was on those cute little faces and their unique presence.

In return, I was rewarded with the cutest smiles and energising childlike laughs. Even the new kid who'd recently started in the same group as my daughter was smiling so nicely back at me after I asked how he was doing. I don't even think that he understood what I was asking him about. But he understood my cheerful face and my soft voice and that made him feel warm and welcoming. I received the best energy ever by simply sharing my smile on that foggy November morning. And I concluded that just in the simple process of walking from the parking lot with my daughter to her day-care, life was beautiful because I watched my little child showing me her friends and telling me her story and I heard the other kids telling me their stories too.

Lesson 39. Our mind is an amazing mechanism. It is so easy to feel happy and to know that life is beautiful. It is beautiful when we want it to be but it is also beautiful if we share a positive vibe. Even on an ordinary winter day. Try it and enjoy it. You won't need any medicine to get your energy level up. The medicine is sharing your smile and your warm presence.

Sharing, at times, might not be as positive and happy as that November morning. Sometimes sharing is a very sensitive process. When you approach this type of sharing, take it seriously and be cautious about how much you wish to share and, most importantly, why you need to share something that is delicate and fragile.

I once had a very delicate private family meeting. It was delicate, not because I needed to clarify many practical matters about a family issue but because I needed to share my emotions and feelings. The meeting went well as long as I was talking about practical matters. It did not go that well when I started sharing my emotions and things that were dear to me. I left the meeting contemplating, whether my sharing was too much for another person to bear. And the answer was yes. It was obvious that I shared things that were hard to hear and it was obvious that some emotions were extremely delicate. I did, however, conclude that it was a must for me to share those feelings because of the values I had. My values and my personal integrity are fundamental parts of who I am. I needed to share my thoughts, so my personal integrity was safeguarded.

The outcome of my sharing was neither a war nor a battlefield on fire. The outcome was silent, where both parties left the meeting and carrying on with their lives. But I felt at ease and I was relieved because I knew that I spoke about my integrity and I made the other person aware of who I was. Nothing in this world is more important than carrying pride and honour for our personal values. No fame, no money, no diamonds can replace personal integrity. Being true to yourself is just like breathing fresh air every second, not feeling dizzy or having to choke. If we are true to our own values, there will always be a way to build a long-term relationship that will only prosper and not deteriorate.

Lesson 40: To share is to live. That is so basic and simple. And that is what makes us and our surroundings happy. Share things with your loved ones. Share your worries. Do think about how you share it. Especially if the matter is very delicate. If your heart is telling you that you must share to sleep well, do that. Just do that gradually and with a smile.

A person once told me, "I would rather share the food with the animals instead of eating alone." How brilliant that thought was and how generous the simple line is: "I would rather share." That person has a good heart. And this simple line made me think about sharing. If we all share and we all commit to good deeds, then we all comfort each other. It makes sense. And that is a recipe for a good life. No matter your culture, in real life all you need is yourself; a person who is capable of loving, sharing, caring and living in good strong relationships.

Lesson 41: Believe in life and believe in yourself. Do not put your focus on theories and do not rely on others. Rely on yourself and the inner power inside of you. Do not try to become someone; become yourself and treat your power with care.

You can never become someone else. I have looked at other people around me and tried to compare myself to them. I wondered why some people are more beautiful or much luckier than I am. Why was I not born into the richest and happiest country? Why do some people have more possibilities than I have? After years of hard work, establishing my life in a completely foreign setting, I understood that it is not a matter of the country where a person is born. Anyone can create their own dream from scratch, even if it is a hard and twisted road. Anyone can build that magic recipe for their own life, not by thinking about wearing a fancy jacket but by sharing that fancy jacket with someone who needs it more.

The Walk

Discovering the timeless power of freedom.

I had a simple watch when I was 20. Without a mobile phone, the watch was a necessity. I had to make it onto a bus to get to work and I had to know the time for my appointments. It was so much easier to know that all that I planned for would fall within the time that the watch around my wrist showed me. I thought that I would fulfil my plans by wearing the watch. One day, though, I forgot to wear my watch and I had a meeting in town that I had to make. I had to go to great lengths that day to make it to that appointment and to prove that my promise is a true promise.

The appointment was scheduled for late evening and I had some spare time to visit my friends during the day. During a chat with my friends in the neighbourhood, one of them said there was a small gathering during the day. So I gladly joined my friends for a small get together. They promised that we would be back in town before evening and I counted the minutes from the time I got to that party to the time I had to be in town. Nobody warned me about where the party was going to take place and, as a teenager, I was very easily fooled. The whole company got into a car and we drove away laughing and talking nonsense. The roads took us farther and farther away from the city. By the time we got to a party, I understood that we were far away from home. I did not like it and I was scared. I was asking if we can go back to the city but everybody thought that I was just a fool and everything was just fine.

I was not a fool and everything was not fine. I wanted to honour my promises and I did not want to be fooled. I had more power inside of me and I had the power to stick to my appointments. Even then in my early teenage development, I had this simple rule: If someone promises you something, then that somebody should stick to the promise. After some hours at the party, I went around asking if we ever were going to get back home to Minsk and the answer was no. I don't exactly know what happened to me the minute I heard the answer. I just said goodbye to my friends and told everyone that I was going to walk home. Alone. Everyone at the party laughed at me and said that I would never have the guts to do that. For them, I was just a naive teenager that would never find the way back home. They thought so. But they were wrong.

I took my jacket and put on my high heels. Some of my friends started telling me that I was stupid and irrational to walk miles back home, not even knowing where I was. A friend who'd promised me that we would go back home to Minsk told me that I needed to relax and have fun. My response was firm and concrete. I said that I needed to make it to my appointment, no matter what and I was true to my promise. I walked out of the house and I hit the darkness. I remember two dogs barking at me so much that I was almost ready to go back to the house. Instead, I took a deep breath and I passed the dogs, not even knowing how far they were away from me and if they were on a leash or not. I ended up walking along a very dark country road. No lights. No cars. Nothing. Just dogs barking and occasionally the voices of people inside of the houses in the villages I passed through. My eyes were watery and I was miserable. I did not know if I should go back or I should continue. I knew that in the dark, I would never find the way back to that house – or the right direction to get home. I was lost. In the dark. I cried. But I kept on going. I thought that I kept on going because I had an important appointment. After many years I realise that it was all about me.

Lesson 42: Do not let anyone scare you. Do not let anyone let you down. Walk with pride, even if your legs hurt, if this is what it takes to get out of a place you hate. Walk and do not be afraid. The darkness and the tears will lead you to the streetlights.

I walked for hours and I did not have my watch with me. I had no sense of direction or time. I just walked because I knew that I needed to continue and that my commitment was higher than the feeling of being fooled and ignored. The pain in my feet was increasing and I stopped to rest because I was exhausted. As I took a break in the darkness, I was scared, not knowing what to do. But I kept on walking. I walked for many hours not knowing the time or the geography or the surroundings.

At last I saw the lights of a big village. I was so relieved that I started crying. The tears of happiness at the fact that I would soon be home, overloaded my face and my teenage heart. I went to the nearest train station and I realised that the night train was about to arrive. I had no money with me but I needed to get home. All I cared about was getting home because I was very late for my appointment. Approaching the train station, I looked at the big clock and I realised that I had walked for six hours in the dark. I did not make it to my scheduled appointment but I was going home. About an hour later I arrived at Minsk central station, took the last bus home and reached my home when it was almost morning. I quietly sneaked into my bedroom, crawled into my warm bed and fell asleep immediately. The next day I woke up and could not move. My legs, my arms and my whole body were aching. I told my parents I was ill and stayed in bed for the entire day. Evening approached and I decided to go over to my friend to tell her how I felt. My friend opened the door and smiled as if nothing had happened. Our conversation was fast. There was nothing left of our friendship but I learned that our values were completely different.

Lesson 43: Our values are who we are. Like a watch, they are a unique mechanism that tells us what we need to do. I did not think of the watch walking home that evening or the time. I tried out my limits and my limits told me a secret: I did not have to use the watch and I did not need it to prove to myself what I am capable of. I learned that I will always walk miles to get to my freedom and my independence.

By 2017, I had not had a watch for almost 20 years. One day in 2017, I had a party with my best friends and we had a frock exchange. My friend had a black box, a watch. I looked at it. I was sceptical but I bought that watch that day. Many days went by before I put the watch on my wrist, contemplating whether I can connect with that old story of mine. I put the watch on my wrist and I took it off immediately. It felt wrong. It bothered my wrist.

Several days went by and I put the watch on again and it felt great. I was not confused anymore. It was a perfect time to say goodbye to the old times when I was fooled. It was time to say hello to a new beginning. At that point, I knew that the watch was a symbol of my power to never give up. The watch did not represent that scared little teenager anymore. The watch represented the powerful and strong woman I had become. The watch meant the evolution of my personality, going from a vulnerable girl to a tough and confident woman. I put the watch back on and left to pick up my daughter and the first thing that she asked me about was the watch that I had on my left wrist. I said that it was a watch and she said she wanted to try it on. My baby, my sweet, sweetest angel. I hope that you will learn from my watch story one day and that no one will fool you as much as I was fooled when I was very young and fragile.

Lesson 44: I understood that it was not about the watch. Neither it was about why I put one on after 20 years. It was all about my teenage stubbornness and willingness to stick to my true self, no matter the time. It was all about the true me 20 years back and 20 years forward. The watch did not change me. The watch made me realise that I have the timeless power to live, love and learn.

The Dreamland

A dream others cannot copy.

For many years I thought that living in Denmark and establishing a happy life from scratch could easily be called a Danish dream. Building my way toward successful living in Denmark, starting as a poor au pair and a student, having no family around and only limited resources to make the right decisions was a tough journey. But I kept on going toward my goals and I kept on believing that one day my life in Denmark would be easy and I would finally feel that I had all that I ever wanted.

I couldn't stop wondering though, if it was a Danish dream that kept me going or if it was some other dream I was living. When I first started contemplating it, I had lived in Denmark for several years and already had many small wins and victories. Still on many occasions I could not resist wondering why I never gave up finding new ambitions and fighting for myself. Was it a dream for a better future or was it something else? I was not sure if I was living a Danish dream or not. I started thinking about what it really took to reach the top of my dreams in Denmark. Out of curiosity, I went on Google and searched for the definition of a Danish dream. Surprisingly, I could hardly find any results. As if no one even speaks about it in Denmark. I looked at the definition of an American dream instead and found dozens of explanations. The clearest and shortest one referred to the fact that life should be better and richer for everyone with the opportunity for each according to ability or achievement regardless of social class or circumstances of birth. I realised my personal beliefs about equal opportunity according to one's ability perfectly matched that statement. However, the first part of the definition about the better and richer life for everyone puzzled me.

I utterly support the thought of a better life for everyone. The only problem was that the word 'should' was not truly syncing with my logic. The 'should' can be related to many personal achievements or the 'should' can be just a notion of a strong welfare system in a country one is born into. For instance in Denmark, the 'should' is rooted in all the beautiful benefits that the social welfare system provides. From the minute one is born into this system, there is always some sort of protection, safety and support. So the 'should' is an embedded element of a better and richer life from birth. In other words, why live a Danish dream if the dream is flying into your arms by default.

Maybe that is why nobody speaks about the notion of a Danish dream because there are no incentives to look for that dream. The dream comes home and knocks at your door but the funny part is that some people choose not to open the door because they are just fine with what society provides for them. Hence, the 'should' is a given lucky coin of a better life in many countries. Searching for an answer about my lucky coin, I had to conclude that my own 'should' was rooted in my ambitions to do whatever it takes to create my own opportunities and my own better and richer life. I also realised that instead of trying for decades to understand why some people do not take any chances to grasp brilliant born-into opportunities, my focus from day one was on reconstructing my life in Denmark through my actions.

Lesson 45: Regardless of a reason for not using great life opportunities, it is easier and, in fact, healthier to just start doing something. Stop wondering why you're not using life opportunities and instead start moving ahead in producing the elements of a better life for yourself.

Theoretically, I could possibly fit into the concept of a Danish dream. I came to Denmark in 2000. I had ten dollars in my pocket, a bag of clothes, a dictionary and a Cambridge self-study book. I could hardly speak English and I had no idea where I was going. My trip was covered by borrowing money and my parents have never approved of my decision. Many years along the way, I have learned English and Danish, gotten Bachelor and Master's degrees at a hot-shot business school and spent many years as a management consultant with a fast-track career path. I became a Dane and was blessed with the greatest gift of all by becoming a mother.

So, yes, I could easily call myself a pure and successful case of living a Danish dream. What got me thinking was this: Did I really need to believe in some theoretical dream to build my life from scratch in Denmark? Did I expect that a belief in a dream was all it would take to build a better future for myself the moment I landed in Denmark? I could only find the answer after very many years of living in Denmark. One day I came home from work and started packing things in big boxes. My apartment was sold and I had to move on to my next life chapter and new residence. I needed to decide what I wanted to bring along to my new home. I realised that almost every single object inside my home was purchased from my own earnings. And it all started with that ten dollars. From that hard work, sleepless nights, frustration and years of living as a poor foreigner. There was my answer – very clearly and concisely.

Lesson 46: I did not rely on any dream concept, so the money and luck would fall from the sky on me. I worked out my own unique way of reaching my own distinct goals in life. All I have today is created by my own hands. My dream is my belief in my strengths that lift me up and fill my life with power.

My own dream turned out extraordinarily well and quickly. I have, of course, experienced many happy and sad moments during the years of reconstructing my life in Denmark but it has been a grand journey of becoming an international citizen. What I realised is that neither the Danish nor American dream brought me a better life. It was my commitment, desire and passion. I strongly believe that every person on this planet has the same capabilities for change. The only difference between our dreams is the content. Every one of us is creating and living a dream every second. The evolution of that dream is truly unique, as unique as each person. A dream can never be reproduced. It will always be personal, distinct and independent.

The power of our own beliefs is much bigger than a belief in theoretical concepts. All of us can reach the sky and touch it. There are many ways of getting what we want. There will, of course, be things that will be hard to handle. And there will definitely be decisions that impact the speed of getting to a desired destination. No matter how tough these decisions are, there is one fact that will always remain unchanged: The fact that each and every one of us is capable of finding a way towards our own real and unique dream.

Lesson 47: Any way and any road can be used to get closer to your own real dream. The keys are quite simple; believe in yourself, stay focused even if you have lost everything dear to you and don't give up. Time will heal all the wounds and time will turn the journey in the right direction. A recipe for creating your dream is you and only you possess that secret power to build your dream from nothing.

The Destination

The only element that will never be missing.

I have written a lot and I needed to connect the story between the chapters. I have read the entire book several times and I was almost ready to say that now I have reached my goal. But on a September morning in 2017, I woke up and found that there was one more essential lesson waiting for me to learn and digest. That morning I had many missed calls from my brother. By the tone of his voice on a voice message, I already knew that I had to prepare for the worst but until the last minute, I cherished a belief that everything was fine at home in Belarus and that my family simply needed my help.

It was early, so instead of calling back immediately I texted my brother, notifying him that I was awake and available. My morning routine went on. I made breakfast for my daughter and started preparing myself for work, knowing that I was just prolonging my belief. I did not hear my phone ringing and suddenly my daughter told me that someone was trying to call me. It was my brother. I called back right away and the first sentence he said was, "Come home." At that minute I knew my father had died.

I made arrangements quickly and booked the flight to Minsk immediately. The time waiting to reach home was painful and I remembered that the evening before that call I could not really fall asleep. I was twisting and turning in my bed. Around 10 p.m. my brother was trying to reach me but my phone was on airplane mode. I heard my daughter calling for me. I clearly heard her. I went to her bedroom but she was sound asleep. I thought that I must have been mistaken and I went to bed. The morning after I understood that I was not mistaken. Exactly at that time, my dad died in a hospital in Minsk. What I heard was a goodbye from my father. Even if this is just a belief I have, it was good for me because I knew that his spirit was near me till his last moment.

I made arrangements for my daughter to stay home in Denmark. I believe that small children should not witness such events. I could tell her later about the funeral but she will always remember her granddad as an alive and cheerful person. While searching for a flight ticket, I battled inside with all my feelings. At some point I did not want to get on a plane and go. I did not want to see my entire family in tears. I did not want to witness the sadness and the darkness of a funeral. I did not want to go. But then I realised that I had exactly the same feeling when my mother died. I was present at the funeral but I never said a proper goodbye to her. It took me decades to get over the feeling of losing her. I didn't want to go through that with losing my dad.

So I bought the ticket and boarded the plane. I was sitting on a plane to Minsk, writing this last chapter and thinking about how I was going to handle my biggest fear again. I knew that lots of tears were just ahead of me and I knew that it would be hard to see my big family in pain. But I kept on thinking that perhaps it was all right. Life and death are unexplainable feelings but all we need is to grieve and cry and we all need to say goodbye at some point to the dearest people on this planet.

Deep inside I knew that this funeral would make me much stronger and change my view on very many things. I knew because it had already happened to me when my mom died and I was only 13. The loss of my father did not feel as heavy because I knew that he was much better off on the other side, resting at peace after years of battling diseases and life's challenges. The last time I saw my father alive was only a month before his death and I could already see that his entire body was in pain. He had worked hard ever since he was 15 on jobs that demanded tough physical activity. His legs were in pain and he died at the age of just 68. His worn and tired body made his last few years very tough and at some point, he gave up. I think he died because he wanted to. Because he wanted the pain to go away. The last time I saw him, he said that he wanted to die but he was not prepared to go away so fast. During that last visit in Minsk, I tried to spend more time with my father. The evening before I had to go back to Denmark, I came to say goodbye to him. We had dinner together and I remembered him saying that he would try to do everything to stay alive. But I think he was protecting me by saying that. Protecting me because he knew that I would be miles away from him and he did not want me to worry about him.

But I did worry. Coming home to Denmark after that last visit, I could not find any peace in my heart. For weeks I called home every day talking to my dad and asking about his well-being. The last phone call and the last time I heard his voice, he was exceptionally happy. He felt much better physically and mentally and he had started walking more. His voice was strong and happy. I told him that I loved him and I told him that I was very proud of him. He raised eight children and had a dozen grandchildren. I said that he is very important to me and I sent a kiss as I said goodbye to him on the phone. This call will always remain in my heart. And this call made me stronger during the funeral because the funeral could never change the things that I told my dad on the phone.

While packing my suitcase, I had to explain to my daughter why I was going away. I tried to explain that her grandfather had been ill for a long time, his heart was weak and that he was tired. But she still kept on asking why. *How can you explain these things to a three-year-old child?* I thought. It was not easy and I used humour. I said that he was a troublemaker and my daughter started smiling. The troublemaker explanation worked and she asked where her grandad's heart was. That was a very nice way of asking about his heart disease. I thought for a minute and then told my daughter that her grandfather's heart was now in mine because I love him unconditionally. She smiled and looked at my chest trying to find her granddad's heart in mine. I felt warm because when people go away, the least we can do is to cherish their hearts in ours and we understand, finally, how much we love them.

Writing these lines on the plane to Minsk, I understood that I was looking forward to saying goodbye to my father at the funeral. And I was looking forward to giving all my love to my family. They will always be around me through every life challenge and event – all of them, funerals or births.

Eternal lesson: Family love sometimes makes us struggle and cry but it also makes us stronger. Parents give us a life, the gift of experiencing all we want. When parents go away, their power and strengths remain with us and those strengths help us establish our own unique dreams. Life challenges will keep happening but as long as we are living and loving our own unique dreams, we have much to look forward to.

List of My Life Lessons

Lesson 1: Don't ignore your childhood wishes and interests.

Lesson 2: Visualise and keep your ideas tuned, so you keep believing in impossible things and staying focused for years.

Lesson 3: Investment in the future and especially investment in your education is the key to a happy and rich life.

Lesson 4: Know your strengths.

Lesson 5: You can be very impatient as a person but once you have a goal, you will not need any tools to train your patience.

Lesson 6: There will be times where you feel completely and utterly alone. Hold on.

Lesson 7: Don't wait for the rain of help to be poured on you from the sky.

Lesson 8: Be bold and take a risk.

Lesson 9: Decisions, effort and the consequences of your actions will show the way to reroute your settings.

Lesson 10: Understanding how we as humans should or should not act is a brilliant lesson.

Lesson 11: Find and cherish the elements of life that make you happy and make sure that you really enjoy them.

Lesson 12: We cannot avoid stressful situations at work; they will happen.

Lesson 13: Do not overreact and create unnecessary drama out of tough moments at work.

Lesson 14: It does not matter what position you have in a company and it does not matter if you have no formal power to change a complicated situation.

Lesson 15: Always think of any job as a means to your self-development.

Lesson 16: When you are in a process of establishing yourself, think big, think options and think smart.

Lesson 17: Always find new goals; small or big.

Lesson 18: When you feel you are about to hit a wall, have a good talk with a dearest friend, your family or a professional therapist.

Lesson 19: Even if you are the strongest person on the planet, cry and feel sorrow for your losses.

Lesson 20: With that experience, I realised that all I needed to get back into normal shape was love.

Lesson 21: When things are too much to bear, you don't owe anything to anyone apart from yourself.

Lesson 22: Do the homework of cleansing your brain.

Lesson 23: Always remember that your body and mind can adjust to any circumstances. It is just a matter of time.

Lesson 24: There is nothing wrong with giving yourself some slack and spending a day doing nothing.

Lesson 25: Don't underestimate the power of colour.

Lesson 26: When you get lazy, enjoy the time but remember to not stop caring about the way you look and the way you feel.

Lesson 27: Try to write down your dreams.

Lesson 28: You don't need to rebuild your night dreams and you don't need to know the concrete meaning behind your dreams.

Lesson 29: We all wish that love would last forever.

Lesson 30: The cure against many dead-end situations is rooted in your personal boundaries.

Lesson 31: Blessing comes rarely and very unexpectedly

Lesson 32: When you feel there is no one around to help and you are alone, find a way to get some sleep and carry on.

Lesson 33: Every parent has one thing in common: responsibility for a child.

Lesson 34: No matter how long it might take for you to understand relationships and family DNA, keep on learning.

Lesson 35: Always accept the good and bad sides that you might discover about your family.

Lesson 36: Your first love and first affection can predict your future story.

Lesson 37: First love is what you least expect to feel in your veins.

Lesson 38: That first love formed a great human being in me.

Lesson 39. Our mind is an amazing mechanism.

Lesson 40: To share is to live.

Lesson 41: Believe in life and believe in yourself.

Lesson 42: Do not let anyone scare you.

Lesson 43: Our values are who we are.

Lesson 44: I understood that it was not about the watch.

Lesson 45: Regardless of a reason for not using great life opportunities, it is easier and, in fact, healthier to just start doing something.

Lesson 46: I did not rely on any dream concept, so the money and luck would fall from the sky on me.

Lesson 47: Any way and any road can be used to get closer to your own real dream.

Eternal lesson: Family love sometimes makes us struggle and cry but it also makes us stronger.